Language Arts

Name _____

Color the pictures that begin with the sound of the letter in front of each row. Put an **X** on the picture that does not belong.

b

d

f

g

h

n

r

t

Language Arts

Name _____

Write the letter with which each picture begins.

___   ___   ___   ___

___   ___   ___   ___

___   ___   ___   ___

___   ___   ___   ___

___   ___   ___   ___

Language Arts

Name _____

In each box, paste the picture that begins with the consonant blend named.

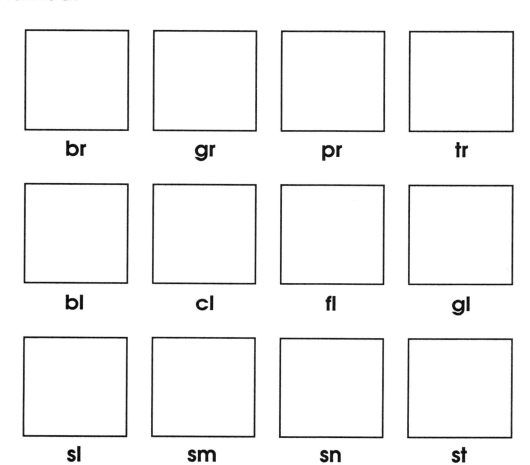

br   gr   pr   tr

bl   cl   fl   gl

sl   sm   sn   st

Language Arts

Name _____

Ch, sh, th, and **wh** are **consonant digraphs**. Write the consonant digraph that begins or ends the word for each picture.

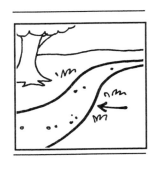

Language Arts

Name _____

Say the name of each picture to yourself. Circle the letter or letters you hear at the **end** of the word.

f   s

g   b

mp   lp

b   d

nt   rt

r   v

s   z

b   k

l   f

t   f

m   l

m   p

Write the ending sound for each word.

do _____

ma _____

gu _____

nai _____

bu _____

mil _____

stam _____

car _____

Language Arts

Name _____

Color the **short a** words **red**.
Color the **long a** words **blue**.

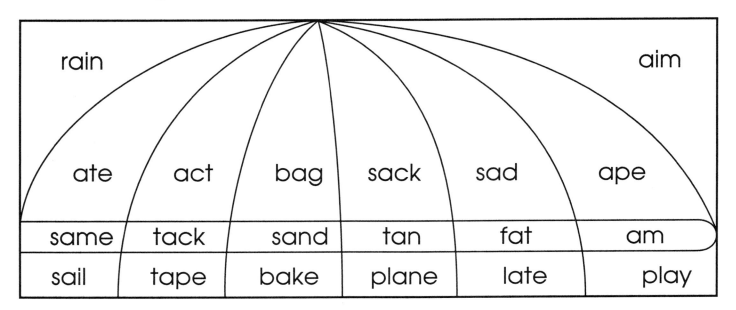

rain					aim
ate	act	bag	sack	sad	ape
same	tack	sand	tan	fat	am
sail	tape	bake	plane	late	play

The hidden picture is a _____ .

Color the **short e** words **yellow**.
Color the **long e** words **green**.

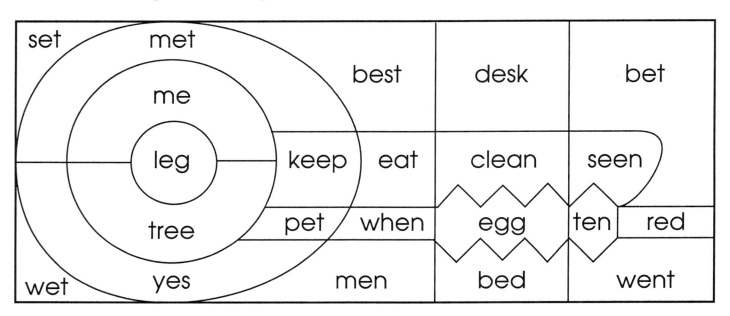

set	met		best	desk	bet
	me				
	leg	keep	eat	clean	seen
		pet	when	egg	ten	red
wet	tree	yes	men	bed	went

The hidden picture is a _____ .

Language Arts

Name _____

Circle each **short i** word. Put a box around each **long i** word.

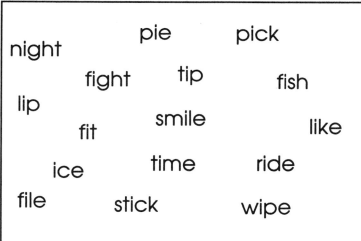

night   pie   pick

fight   tip   fish

lip

smile   like

fit

ice   time   ride

file   stick   wipe

Draw a line from each picture to the words that have the same vowel sound.

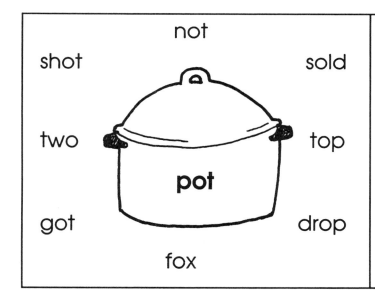

not

shot   sold

two   top

pot

got   drop

fox

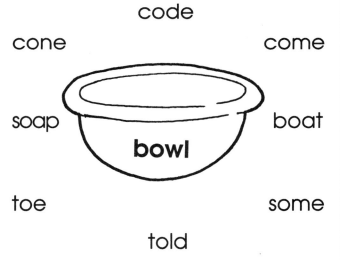

code

cone   come

soap   boat

bowl

toe   some

told

Underline each **short u** word with one line. Underline each **long u** word with two lines.

cube   tube   flute   use

pup   mule   true   cub

must   bull   us   thumb

Language Arts

Name _____

If the words on a pair of socks rhyme, color the socks. If they do not, put an **X** on the socks.

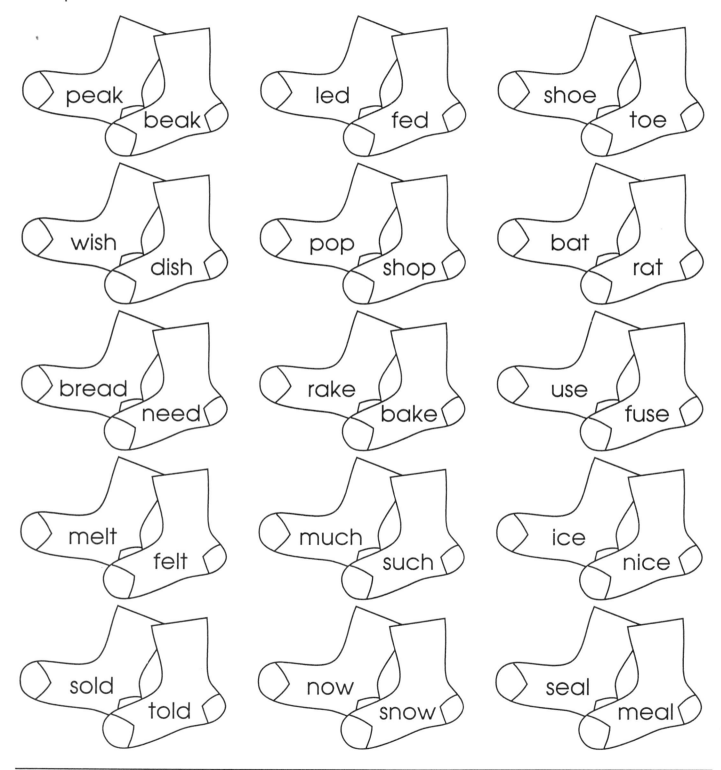

Language Arts

Name _____

Synonyms are words that mean nearly the same thing. **Gift** and **present** are synonyms.

Look at the picture below. If a pair of words are **synonyms**, color the space **red**. If they are not, color the space **green**.

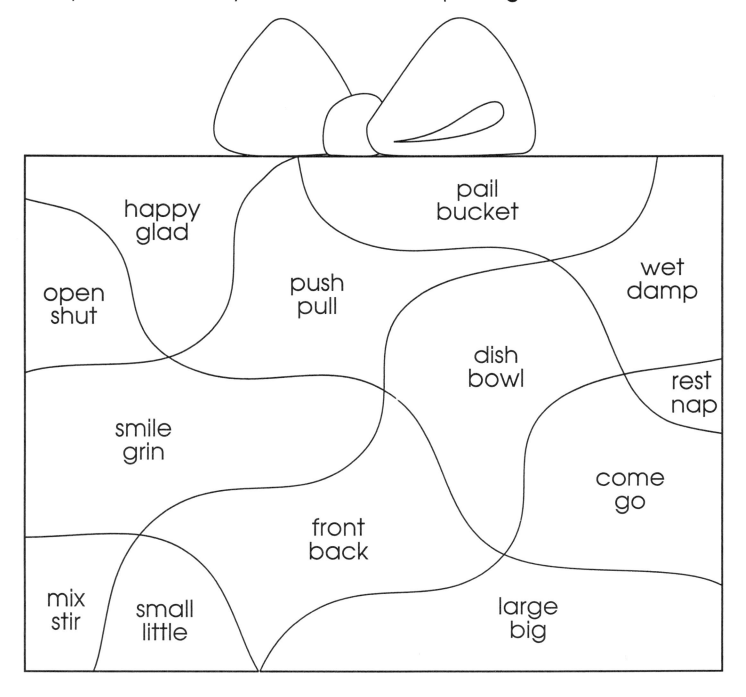

Language Arts

Name _____

Find a word from the Word Box that is the **opposite** of the word on a bubble.

bottom _____

happy _____

win _____

summer _____

fat _____

night _____

short _____

lost _____

down _____

work _____

Word Box

| top | found | play | up | winter |
| tall | lose | thin | day | sad |

Language Arts

Name _____

Write a word from the Word Box to complete each sentence correctly.

1. **Wing** is to **bird** as **fin** is to _____ .

2. **Boat** is to **ship** as **stone** is to _____ .

3. **Hive** is to **bee** as **barn** is to _____ .

4. **Give** is to **take** as **hot** is to _____ .

5. **Toe** is to **foot** as **finger** is to _____ .

6. **Coat** is to **jacket** as **smile** is to _____ .

7. **Snow** is to **snowy** as **sun** is to _____ .

8. **Come** is to **go** as **start** is to _____ .

9. **Take** is to **took** as **see** is to _____ .

10. **Tap** is to **tape** as **hat** is to _____ .

Word Box

cold	cow	fish	grin	hand
hate	rock	saw	stop	sunny

Language Arts

Name _____

Put an **X** on the word in each list that does not belong. Write a word from the Word Box that does belong in the list.

pencil paper parrot books crayons	horse cow chicken chuckle pig	summer mother father brother sister
banana apple orange pear pickle	Thursday Tuesday Friday Frosty Monday	purple paint red green blue
October Mars March July September	walk run jump sleep skip	John Bill Carmen Ashley Ohio

Word Box
May	leap	aunt	George	ruler
sheep	yellow	Sunday	grape	

Language Arts

Name _____

Number the pictures in the correct order.

_____   _____   _____   _____

Read the story.

> Joel got his backpack. He opened it and took
> out his spelling book. Joel went to his desk.
> He wrote his spelling words two times each.

Underline which happened **first**.

a. Joel went to his desk.
b. Joel took out his book.

Underline which happened **last**.

a. Joel wrote his spelling words.
b. Joel opened his backpack.

Number the sentences in the correct order.

_____ Kate cut out many shapes.

_____ Kate mixed the dough.

_____ Kate put the cookies on the cookie sheet.

_____ She rolled out the dough.

_____ She baked the cookies.

Language Arts

Name _____

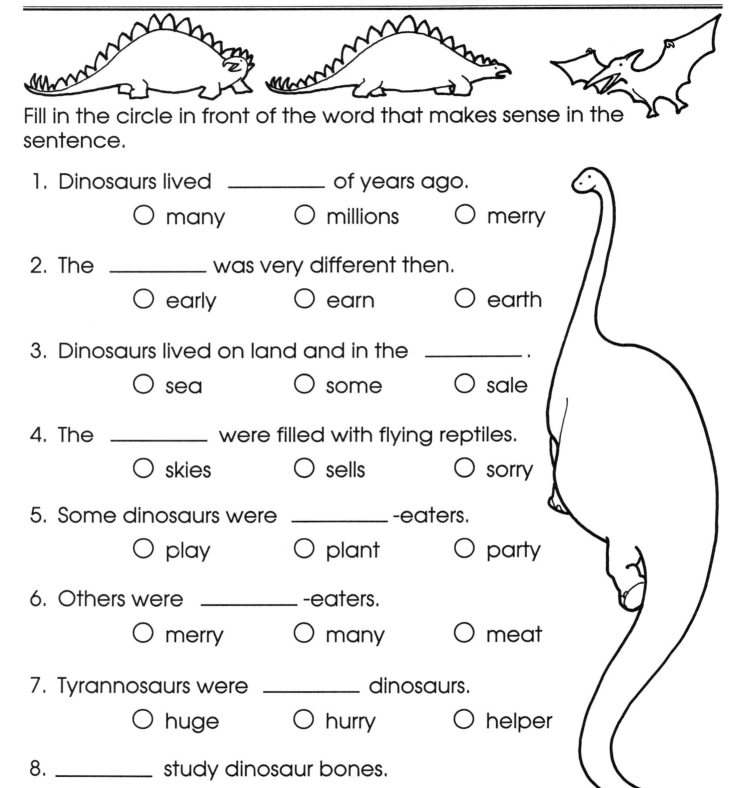

Fill in the circle in front of the word that makes sense in the sentence.

1. Dinosaurs lived _____ of years ago.
   ○ many   ○ millions   ○ merry

2. The _____ was very different then.
   ○ early   ○ earn   ○ earth

3. Dinosaurs lived on land and in the _____ .
   ○ sea   ○ some   ○ sale

4. The _____ were filled with flying reptiles.
   ○ skies   ○ sells   ○ sorry

5. Some dinosaurs were _____ -eaters.
   ○ play   ○ plant   ○ party

6. Others were _____ -eaters.
   ○ merry   ○ many   ○ meat

7. Tyrannosaurs were _____ dinosaurs.
   ○ huge   ○ hurry   ○ helper

8. _____ study dinosaur bones.
   ○ Scientists   ○ Sundays   ○ Summer

Language Arts

Draw a line from each **effect** to its **cause** to make a complete sentence.

Effect

Cause

1. Max put on his boots because . . .

   a. she was late.

2. Dad opened the window because . . .

   b. it was snowing.

3. Samantha ran to the bus stop because . . .

   c. it was hungry.

4. Juan fed the dog because . . .

   d. his room was hot.

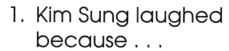

1. Kim Sung laughed because . . .

   a. he had fallen down.

2. Pedro turned out the light because . . .

   b. it needed to be baked.

3. Alex's knee hurt because . . .

   c. the joke was funny.

4. Mom put the pie in the oven because . . .

   d. it was bedtime.

Language Arts

Name _____

Read each story carefully. Circle the picture that answers the question.

Rita saw many birds. Some were in the pine trees. Others were diving for fish. Where was Rita?

Alex got out his books. Then he hung his jacket in the locker he shared with Sam. Where was Alex?

Monica sat by the window. She looked at everything rushing by. She saw a tunnel ahead. Where was Monica?

Cory bought a ticket. He went inside to see the picture. He sat in the dark. Where was Cory?

Mark pushed a cart as he walked up and down the aisles. Finally, he found the box of cereal he wanted. Where was Mark?

Katie liked to visit the animals. She enjoyed feeding them. She gave the chickens some grain. Where was Katie?

Language Arts

Name _____

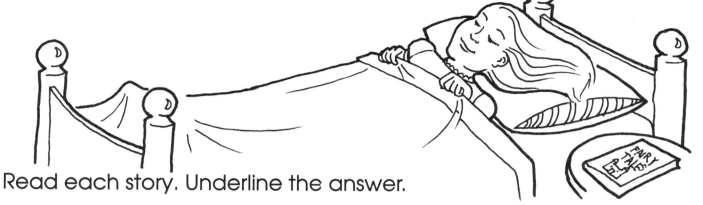

Read each story. Underline the answer.

Sheri put her book aside. She
pulled up the covers. She
turned out the light.

What will Sheri do next?
   a. read her book
   b. go to sleep

Marvin stood in line. He got
a tray of food. Marvin paid
for his meal.

What will Marvin do next?
   a. watch a movie
   b. eat lunch

The doors opened. People got
off. Chelsea got on. The doors
closed.

What will Chelsea do next?
   a. ride the bus
   b. start to cry

Dale heard the siren. He saw
the flashing lights. He heard
the roar of the truck.

What will Dale do next?
   a. call the fire station
   b. get out of the way

Rita put on a life jacket. She
stepped aboard. She saw the
sails fill with wind.

What will Rita do next?
   a. ride on a sailboat
   b. swim in a swimming pool

Language Arts

Name _____

In each story, underline the main idea sentence. Then, write one detail sentence on the lines below.

Many different animals live in a tropical rain forest. Sloths and lemurs live there. Huge moths live there, too.

_____

_ _

Koalas are mammals. They live in Australia. They sleep during the day. They eat leaves at night. The mother koala carries her baby in her pouch. Koalas are unusual animals.

_____

_ _

Some animals have stripes to help protect them. Chipmunks have stripes. So do tigers and zebras. Even some caterpillars have stripes.

_____

_ _

Language Arts

Name _____

Add -**s** to a verb that tells what one person, animal, or thing does. Do not add -**s** to verbs that tell what two or more people, animals, or things do.

Write the correct verb.

1. Teddy _____ to go to the pet store.
(want, wants)

2. He _____ Mom to take him.
(ask, asks)

3. Mom and Teddy _____ into the car.
(get, gets)

4. They _____ to the mall.
(drive, drives)

5. Teddy _____ ahead to the store.
(run, runs)

6. He _____ just what he wants.
(see, sees)

7. A puppy with sad eyes _____ up at Teddy.
(look, looks)

8. Teddy _____ the little dog.
(hug, hugs)

Language Arts

Name _____

An **adjective** describes or tells about a noun. Number words and color words are adjectives.

Color the spaces with number words yellow. Color the spaces with color words green. If the word is not an adjective, color the space blue.

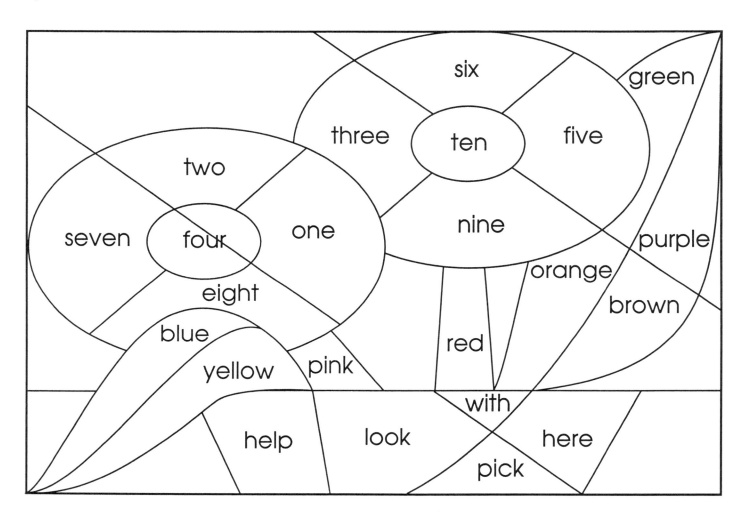

Circle the adjectives in the story.

Ben picked three flowers for Mother. Two flowers were tulips. They were red and pink. One flower was a daisy. The daisy was yellow.

Language Arts

Name _____

An **adjective** describes or tells about a noun. Choose an adjective from the Word Box to describe each noun pictured below.

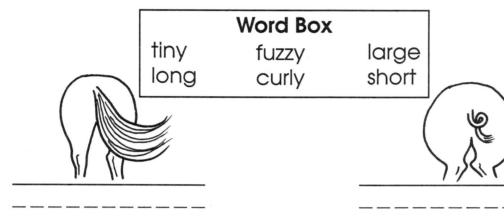

Word Box

tiny	fuzzy	large
long	curly	short

1. a _____ tail

4. a _____ tail

2. _____ ears

5. the _____ cow

3. a _____ chick

6. the _____ mouse

Circle the adjective in each phrase. Underline the noun it describes.

1. the soft kitten

4. a loud rooster

2. the little duckling

5. the lovely swan

3. the funny goat

6. the strong ox

Language Arts

Name _____

Add **-er** to most **adjectives** to compare two things. Add **-est** to most **adjectives** to compare more than two things.

Write the correct adjective in each sentence.

1. This is the _____ dog show in the world.
   (bigger, biggest)

2. Bart's dog is _____ than Brett's dog.
   (bigger, biggest)

3. Miguel's poodle is _____ than Mindy's.
   (smaller, smallest)

4. Do you think it is the _____ poodle of all?
   (smaller, smallest)

5. No, Suzie's poodle is _____ than Mindy's.
   (tinier, tiniest)

6. It is the _____ dog I've ever seen.
   (tinier, tiniest)

7. That collie is _____ than a bulldog.
   (prettier, prettiest)

8. It's the _____ dog here.
   (prettier, prettiest)

Language Arts

Name _____

A **sentence** is a group of words that tells a complete idea.

Write **S** on the bear if the group of words makes a sentence. Draw an **X** on the bear if it does not.

1. There are many kinds of bears.

2. My favorite is the polar bear.

3. A polar bear lives where it is very cold.

4. It hunts for seals.

5. Seals must have air to breathe.

6. Waits by a hole in the ice.

7. Then the polar bear catches the seal.

8. With its strong claws.

9. A polar bear has a white fur coat.

10. The white fur helps the bear hide.

Language Arts

Name _____

The **subject** of a sentence tells who or what does something.
Underline the subject of each sentence.

1. Carlos and Rita went to the circus yesterday.

2. The funny clowns made them laugh.

3. The lion tamer was very brave.

4. A white horse carried six people on its back.

5. Two lovely girls walked a tightrope.

6. An elephant picked up a man with its trunk.

7. The tigers leaped through hoops.

8. One man was shot out of a cannon.

9. The band played loud circus music.

10. The children ate peanuts and cotton candy.

11. The family had a great time.

12. The circus won't be back until next year.

Draw a picture of a circus.

Language Arts

Name _____

The **predicate** of a sentence tells what the subject **is** or **does**.
Underline the predicate of the sentence with two lines.

1. My family helps save the earth.

2. We recycle aluminum cans.

3. I smash the cans for Dad.

4. We try not to use much paper.

5. My mother cleans with rags.

6. I use both sides of a sheet of paper.

7. I take a lunch box to school instead of a paper sack.

8. We collect old newspapers to recycle.

9. The family is careful with water.

10. We shower instead of taking a bath.

11. Dad fixes leaky faucets.

12. We turn out lights when we can.

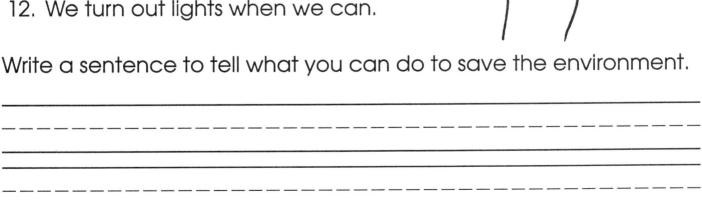

Write a sentence to tell what you can do to save the environment.

_____

_____

_____

_____

Language Arts

Name _____

A **statement** is a sentence that tells something. It begins with a **capital letter** and ends with a period. Write each sentence correctly.

1. george Washington was born in 1732

   _____

   _____

2. he grew up in Virginia

   _____

   _____

3. his father owned a big farm

   _____

   _____

4. George became a surveyor

   _____

   _____

5. he drew maps of the land

   _____

   _____

6. George joined the army

   _____

   _____

7. he became a general

   _____

   _____

Language Arts

Name _____

A **question** is a sentence that asks something. It begins with a **capital letter** and ends with a **question mark**.

If the sentence asks a question, add a question mark and color the top hat black. If it does not ask a question, draw an **X** on the top hat.

 1. Was Abraham Lincoln born in 1809

 2. He lived in Kentucky for awhile

3. Did his family move to Indiana

  4. Can you remember his sister's name

  5. Could it have been Sarah

6. Abe's mother died when he was young

 7. When did Abe move to Illinois

  8. Are you sure he became a lawyer

  9. When did he become President

Draw a picture of Abraham Lincoln's log cabin.

Language Arts

Name _____

A **statement** is a sentence that tells something. A **question** is a sentence that asks something.

Change the word order to make each statement into a question and make each question into a statement. Write the new sentence on the line. Remember to begin each sentence with a capital letter and use the correct end mark.

1. Have you read about Pecos Bill?

   _____

   _____

2. "Pecos Bill" is a tall tale.

   _____

   _____

3. Bill did get lost from his parents.

   _____

   _____

4. Was Bill raised by coyotes?

   _____

   _____

5. Did Bill think he was a coyote?

   _____

   _____

6. Bill was told he was a Texan.

   _____

   _____

Language Arts

Name _____

A special name for a person or a pet begins with a **capital letter**.
Write each name correctly on the line.

jane

1. _____

steven

4. _____

fluffy

2. _____

erica

5. _____

pete

3. _____

buster

6. _____

Fill in the circle below the word if the word should begin with a capital letter.

1. Yesterday judy and I took our dog to the vet.
   ○   ○   ○

2. We saw suzie there with her cat, muffin.
   ○   ○   ○   ○

3. The kitten and sparky chased each other.
   ○   ○   ○   ○

Language Arts

Name _____

Begin a person's **first, middle**, and **last name** with a **capital letter**. An **initial** also begins with a capital letter. Write each name correctly.

sue ann lewis

1. _____

emily jeffers

2. _____

juan mendoza

3. _____

barry w. churchill

4. _____

billy buford

5. _____

mike lopez

6. _____

kim lee tran

7. _____

carol kruger

8. _____

Begin titles such as **Mr., Mrs., Ms.** and **Miss** with **capital letters**. Write each name correctly.

mr. george jones

1. _____

miss mary smith

2. _____

ms. j. r. treadwell

3. _____

mr. and mrs. carlson

4. _____

Language Arts

Name _____

The name of a **special place** begins with a **capital letter**. Write the name of each special place correctly. Use the Word Box.

Word Box

city hall   forest park   green's market
buder school   game land   modern museum
oakland station   denver zoo

1. _____

2. _____

3. _____

4. _____

5. _____

6. _____

7. _____

8. _____

Language Arts

Name _____

Begin the name of a street with a capital letter. If the word street, road, drive, court, or avenue is used with the street's name, capitalize it also. **Examples:** Market Street, Berry Road

Write the street names correctly.

1. turner avenue _____

2. appleton court _____

3. drexel drive _____

4. tenth street _____

5. forest road _____

The name of a state begins with a capital letter. Write the names correctly.

1. alaska _____   4. florida _____

2. maine _____   5. oregon _____

3. kentucky _____   6. wyoming _____

Write the name of your state. _____

Language Arts

Name _____

The name of each **day** of the week and **month** of the year begins with a **capital letter**.

Write each day and month correctly.

1. wednesday _____

2. february _____

3. sunday _____

4. august _____

5. saturday _____

6. april _____

7. tuesday _____

Names for **special days** and **holidays** begin with **capital letters**.
Fill in the circle of the correctly written special day or holiday.

1. ○ christmas eve
   ○ Christmas Eve

2. ○ Groundhog day
   ○ Groundhog Day

3. ○ Hanukkah
   ○ hanukkah

4. ○ Independence day
   ○ Independence Day

5. ○ Mother's Day
   ○ mother's Day

6. ○ Thanksgiving
   ○ thanksgiving

Language Arts

Name _____

Use a **period** at the end of a **statement** or after an **abbreviation**.
Write the word or initial that should be followed by a period. Add the period.

1. Mr Hall came to visit my classroom. _____

2. They came to talk about our city _____

3. I live in St Louis. _____

4. Some streets were named for famous people _____

5. One was named for Charles A. Lindbergh _____

Write the abbreviation for each word. Use the Word Box.

Word Box			
Dr.	Mr.	Sept.	Mon.
Nov.	Rd.	Ave.	St.

1. Mister _____

2. Street _____

3. Monday _____

4. Avenue _____

5. Doctor _____

6. Road _____

7. September _____

8. November _____

Language Arts

Name _____

Use a **question mark** after a sentence that asks a question.
If the sentence asks a question, color the tooth and add the
question mark. If it does not, draw an **X** on the tooth.

 1. Have you ever been to the dentist

 2. Were you afraid to go

 3. Do you brush your teeth twice a day

 4. Can you use floss correctly

 5. The dentist can show you how

 6. Did you have any cavities

 7. I go to the dentist twice a year

Write each question correctly.

1. Have you lost any teeth

Yes

2. How many have you lost

3. Can you name the back teeth

Do

Language Arts

Name _____

Use a **comma** to separate the day and the year in a date.
Write the dates correctly. **Example:** March 1**,** 1995.

May 6 1993

1. _____

December 21 1996

2. _____

September 10 1995

3. _____

October 31 1994

4. _____

April 1 1991

5. _____

February 2 1994

6. _____

Use a **comma** to separate a **city** and **state**.
Write the cities and states correctly. **Example:** Akron**,** Ohio

Columbus Ohio

1. _____

Chicago Illinois

2. _____

Miami Florida

3. _____

Dallas Texas

4. _____

Atlanta Georgia

5. _____

Hope Arkansas

6. _____

Language Arts

Name _____

A friendly letter has a **date**, **greeting**, **body**, **closing**, and **signature**.

(date) → March 7, 1995

Dear Aunt Molly, ← **(greeting)**

(body) → { Thank you for inviting me to meet you in Topeka. I will be happy to see you again.

Love, ← **(closing)**

Megan ← **(signature)**

Copy the letter correctly on these lines.

_____

_____

_____

_____

_____

_____

_____

_____

_____

_____

_____

_____

_____

1. What is the date on the letter? _____

2. Who wrote the letter? _____

Language Arts

Name _____

A **paragraph** has a sentence that tells the **main idea**. All the other sentences in a paragraph must tell about the main idea.

Read the paragraph. Draw a line through the sentence that does not tell about the main idea.

Unusual plants and animals live in the desert. Hairy tarantulas live there. My family drove through the desert. Saguaro cactuses grow in the desert.

A paragraph is written in a special form. The first sentence is **indented**. The other sentences follow each other. Write the sentences below in **paragraph form**. Leave out the sentence that does not tell about the main idea.

Pandas are interesting animals.
They are not bears.
They belong to the raccoon family.
Pandas live in China.

They have woolly black and white fur.
People in China eat rice.
Bamboo shoots are their favorite food.

Language Arts

Name _____

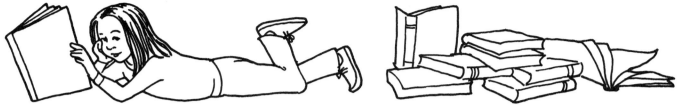

Fill in this form to tell about a book you have read.

Book Title: _____

Author: _____

Illustrator: _____

Check one. This book was: **fiction** _____ **non-fiction** _____ .

This book was mainly about _____

_____

The part I liked best was _____

_____

Write some new words from the book.

1. _____   3. _____

2. _____   4. _____

Circle one.   This book was . . .   **great**   **okay**   **terrible**

Language Arts

Name _____

A **cinquain** is a form of poetry.
It follows a special pattern.

Example:

Line 1: a noun

Line 2: two adjectives to
describe the noun

Line 3: three -ing verbs

Line 4: four words that tell
something special
about the noun

Line 5: synonym for the noun
or repeat line one

Butterfly

orange, black

soaring, floating, gliding

darts among the flowers

monarch

On the lines below, write a cinquain about a dinosaur.

_____
_____
_____
_____
_____
_____
_____
_____
_____
_____

Math

Name _____

Circle how many.

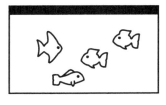

3   4   5

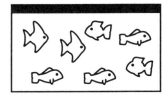

6   7   8

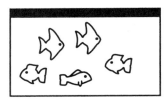

5   6   7

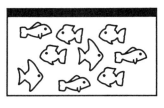

7   8   9

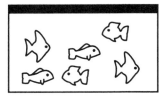

4   5   6

0   1   2

Write how many.

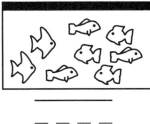

_____
_ _ _ _
_____

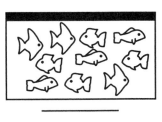

_____
_ _ _ _
_____

_____
_ _ _ _
_____

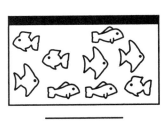

_____
_ _ _ _
_____

Write the missing numbers.

0 ___ ___ ___ 4 ___ ___ ___ ___ ___ 10

Math

Name _____

Count a set of gum balls. Cut and paste it on the correct machine.

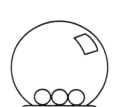 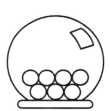 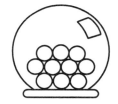

Math

Name _____

Write each time.

_____ o'clock

_____ o'clock

_____ o'clock

_____ o'clock

_____ o'clock

_____ o'clock

Write each time.

___ : ___

___ : ___

___ : ___

Draw each hour hand.

4:00

11:00

9:00

2:00

Math

Name _____

Write each time.

___:___   ___:___   ___:___

___:___   ___:___   ___:___

Draw each minute hand.

__1:30__   __3:30__   __8:00__

__4:00__   __2:30__   __10:30__

Write each time.

___:___   ___:___

one hour before   one hour later

Math

Name _____

Write the subtraction sentences.

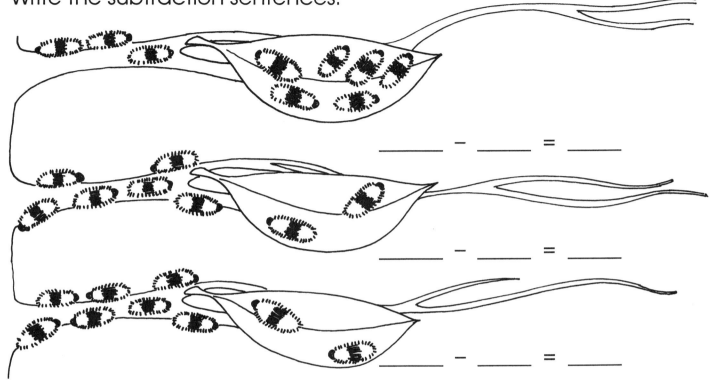

_____ – _____ = _____

_____ – _____ = _____

_____ – _____ = _____

Subtract.

13 – 8 = ____	18 – 9 = ____	15 – 8 = ____
10 – 5 = ____	17 – 8 = ____	12 – 9 = ____
15 – 9 = ____	13 – 9 = ____	16 – 9 = ____
12 – 6 = ____	16 – 7 = ____	13 – 6 = ____
14 – 9 = ____	16 – 8 = ____	10 – 6 = ____
14 – 8 = ____	17 – 9 = ____	13 – 5 = ____

Math

Name _____

Solve.

6 +	
6 =	_____
3 =	_____
9 =	_____
4 =	_____
8 =	_____
2 =	_____

16 −	
9 =	_____
5 =	_____
6 =	_____
3 =	_____
8 =	_____
2 =	_____

13 −	
8 =	_____
5 =	_____
9 =	_____
7 =	_____
3 =	_____
4 =	_____

8 +	
7 =	_____
1 =	_____
9 =	_____
6 =	_____
4 =	_____
2 =	_____
8 =	_____

18 −	
9 =	_____
4 =	_____
1 =	_____
8 =	_____
5 =	_____
7 =	_____
3 =	_____

7 +	
9 =	_____
1 =	_____
8 =	_____
7 =	_____
2 =	_____
5 =	_____
4 =	_____

Math

Name _____

Write two addition and two subtraction facts for each number family.

7, 9, 16

___ + ___ = ___
___ + ___ = ___
___ − ___ = ___
___ − ___ = ___

7, 8, 15

___ + ___ = ___
___ + ___ = ___
___ − ___ = ___
___ − ___ = ___

8, 9, 17

___ + ___ = ___
___ + ___ = ___
___ − ___ = ___
___ − ___ = ___

5, 9, 14

___ + ___ = ___
___ + ___ = ___
___ − ___ = ___
___ − ___ = ___

5, 8, 13

___ + ___ = ___
___ + ___ = ___
___ − ___ = ___
___ − ___ = ___

6, 9, 15

___ + ___ = ___
___ + ___ = ___
___ − ___ = ___
___ − ___ = ___

5, 7, 12

___ + ___ = ___
___ + ___ = ___
___ − ___ = ___
___ − ___ = ___

6, 7, 13

___ + ___ = ___
___ + ___ = ___
___ − ___ = ___
___ − ___ = ___

Math

Name _____

Write the addition or subtraction sentence.

You had 6 🪙 You earned 5 🪙 How many cents do you have in all? ___ ¢	You had 8 🪙 You found 6 🪙 How many cents do you have in all? ___ ¢
You had 15 🪙 You lost 6 🪙 How many cents do you have left? ___ ¢	You had 13 🪙 You gave away 7 🪙 How many cents do you have left? ___ ¢
You bought 8 🍎 You bought 9 🍊 How many in all? ___	You bought 12 🍌 You ate 7 🍌 How many do you have left? ___
You saw 13 🍎 6 were red. How many were not red? ___	You bought 9 🍐 You bought 6 more. How many did you buy in all? ___
You picked 7 🌸 You picked 8 more 🌼 How many did you pick all together? ___	You bought 14 🍭 You ate 5 🍭 How many do you have left? ___

Health and Science

Name _____

Make wise food choices by using the food group pyramid. Study the pyramid. Complete the exercises.

Write.

1. How many servings of fruits should you eat daily? _____

2. How many servings of vegetables should you eat daily? _____

3. Of what group should you eat the most?
_____
_____
_____

Circle.

4. In which group are eggs?   milk and cheese   meat and nuts

5. In which group is candy?   fats, oils, and sweets   fruits

Plan a healthy lunch. Draw pictures of foods to pack in the lunch box.

© Instructional Fair, Inc.

IF8783 First Grade in Review

Health and Science

Name _____

Write a sentence to tell about something you remember doing as a baby.

_____

- -

_____

Write about something you can do now.

_____

- -

_____

Cut and paste the pictures below to answer the questions.

a. What could a baby do?

b. What could a child do?

c. What could an adult do?

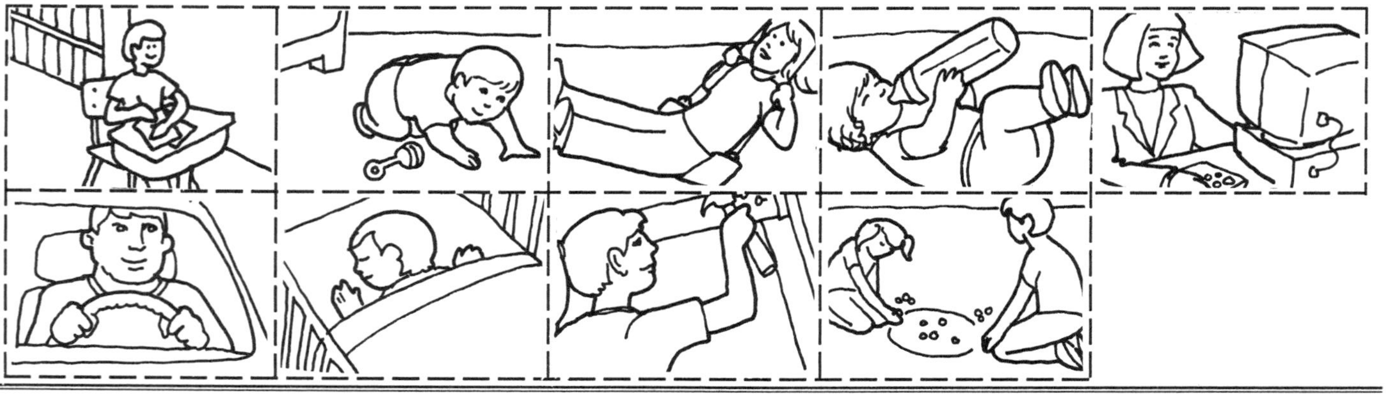

Health and Science

Name _____

Write the name of the home in which each animal lives. Use the words from the Word Box.

 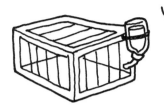 

Word Box			
tree	woods	ocean	den
cage	burrow	nest	hive

1. bear   ___ ___ ___

2. whale   ___ ___ ___ ___ ___

3. hamster   ___ ___ ___ ___

4. bee   ___ ___ ___

5. deer   ___ ___ ___ ___

6. groundhog   ___ ___ ___ ___ ___ ___

7. bird   ___ ___ ___ ___

8. squirrel   ___ ___ ___ ___

Write the letters in order from the top of the box down. You will name a home for a puppy.

___ ___ ___ ___ ___ ___ ___ ___

Health and Science

Name _____

Color each picture that shows a way to help the environment.
Draw an **X** on those that do not.

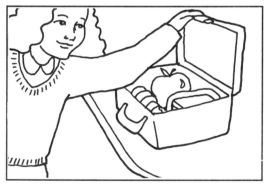

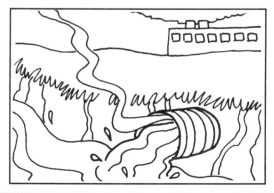

Health and Science

Name _____

Draw a line to match the words with the correct picture.

1. A butterfly lays an egg on a leaf.

2. A caterpillar comes out of the egg. It eats and eats.

3. The caterpillar spins a cocoon. Inside, the caterpillar becomes a pupa.

4. A butterfly comes out of the cocoon. It dries its wings and flies away.

Cut and paste the pictures on the circle in the correct order to show the life cycle of a butterfly.

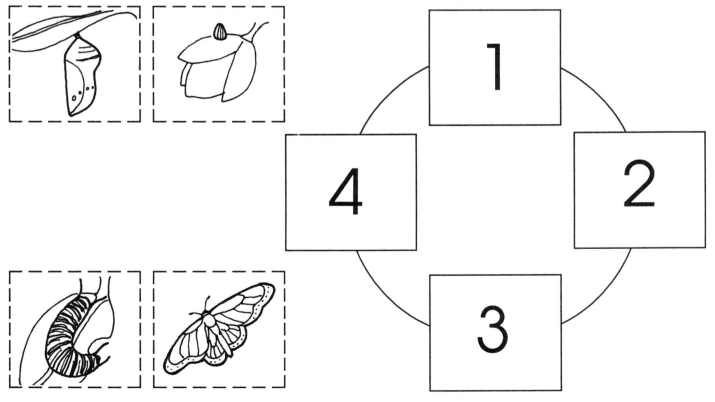

Health and Science

Name _____

Match the pictures on the left with those on the right to show how heat changes things.

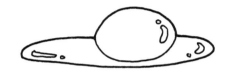

Health and Science

Name _____

Color the picture in each set that shows a way to be safe. Draw an **X** on the one that is not safe.

 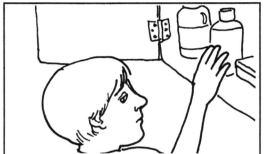

Health and Science

Name _____

Read the sentence strips at the bottom of the page. Cut and paste them in the correct order on the lines.

_____

_____

_____

_____

The baby plant sprouts.

The plant grows taller and ears of corn form.

The seed of corn is planted in good soil.

The ears of corn are ready to pick.

Social Studies

Name _____

Use the Word Box to write the names of family members.

Word Box		
mother	sister	grandpa
father	brother	grandma

_____

_____

_____

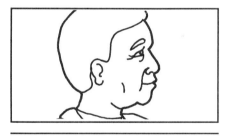

_____

_____

_____

Color the pictures that show how family members help each other.

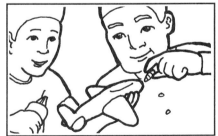

Social Studies

Name _____

All people **need** food, clothing, shelter, and love. Sometimes people **want** other things as well.

Draw a line through the row that shows three things people **need**.

Write **want** or **need** after each word.

1. jeans _____

2. sweater _____

3. hugs _____

4. shoes _____

5. wagon _____

6. family _____

7. home _____

8. violin _____

9. milk _____

10. candy _____

Social Studies

Name _____

Write the name of the worker under the picture. Use the Word Box.

Word Box

farmer	painter	teacher
pilot	nurse	bus driver

_ _ _ _ _ _ _ _ _ _ _ _ _

_ _ _ _ _ _ _ _ _ _ _ _ _

_ _ _ _ _ _ _ _ _ _ _ _ _

_ _ _ _ _ _ _ _ _ _ _ _ _

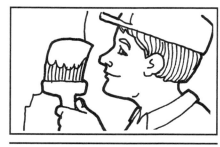

_ _ _ _ _ _ _ _ _ _ _ _ _

_ _ _ _ _ _ _ _ _ _ _ _ _

Complete the sentences.

When I grow up, I want to be a _____ .

I will work in _____ .

Social Studies

Name _____

In the boxes below, **color** only the pictures of **groups**.

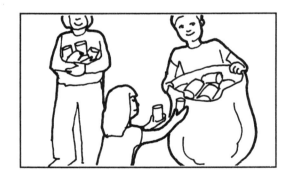

Rules help groups work together. Check the rules that help groups work together.

_____ 1. Take turns talking.   _____ 4. Everyone talk at once.

_____ 2. Listen carefully.   _____ 5. Share the work.

_____ 3. Share ideas.   _____ 6. Be polite.

Social Studies

Name _____

Read the chart to find out how Abraham Lincoln and John F. Kennedy were alike and different. Use the information to answer the questions.

Abraham Lincoln

was poor as a child

loved to read

had a good sense of humor

the father of three sons

became President of the U.S.

was shot and killed

John F. Kennedy

was rich as a child

loved to read

had a good sense of humor

the father of a boy and a girl

became President of the U.S.

was shot and killed

1. In how many ways were Abraham Lincoln and John F. Kennedy alike? _____

2. Which man was rich as a child? _____

3. Which man had more children? _____

4. Which man had a daughter? _____

Write the name of the person who is President now.

_____

_____

Social Studies

Name _____

Holidays are special days which some people celebrate. Match the picture with the name of the holiday.

Hanukkah

Christmas

Halloween

Fourth of July

Thanksgiving

Martin Luther King, Jr. Day

Easter

Write two sentences about a holiday you celebrate.

_____

_____

_____

Answer Key
First Grade
in Review

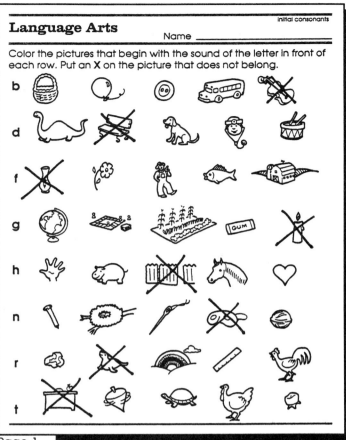

Page 1

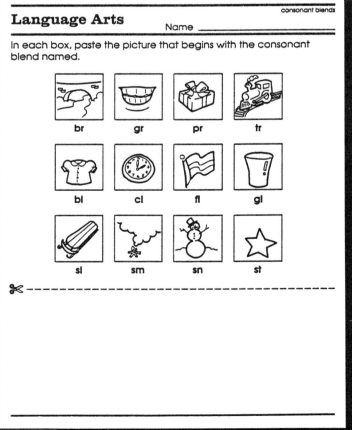

Page 2

Page 3

Language Arts

Name _____

Ch, sh, th, and **wh** are **consonant digraphs.** Write the consonant digraph that begins or ends the word for each picture.

sh   ch   sh   th

ch   sh   ch   th

sh   wh   ch   sh

ch   th   wh   sh

Page 4

Language Arts

Name _____

Say the name of each picture to yourself. Circle the letter or letters you hear at the **end** of the word.

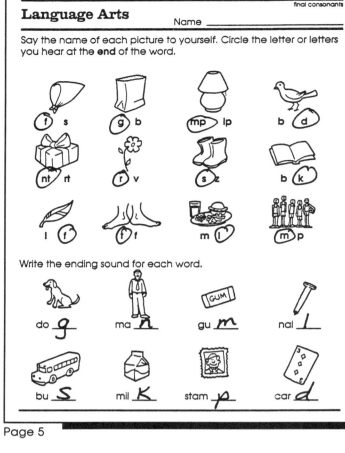

Write the ending sound for each word.

do _g_   ma ___   gu _m_   nai _l_

bu _s_   mil _k_   stam _p_   car _d_

Page 5

Language Arts

Name _____

Color the **short a** words **red.**
Color the **long a** words **blue.**

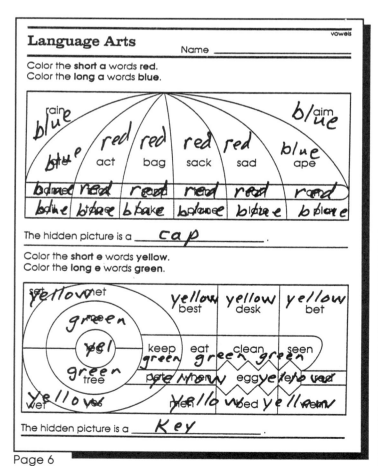

blue   rain   blue   aim
blue   red   red   red   red   blue
act   bag   sack   sad   ape
blue   red   red   red   red   red
blue   blue   blue   blue   blue   blue

The hidden picture is a ___cap___.

Color the **short e** words **yellow.**
Color the **long e** words **green.**

yellow   net   yellow   yellow   yellow
green   best   desk   bet
yel
green   tree   keep   eat   clean   seen
green   green   green
yellow   net   hen   egg   yellow   red
wet
yellow   yellow   red   yellow   men

The hidden picture is a ___Key___.

Page 6

Language Arts

Name _____

Circle each **short i** word. Put a box around each **long i** word.

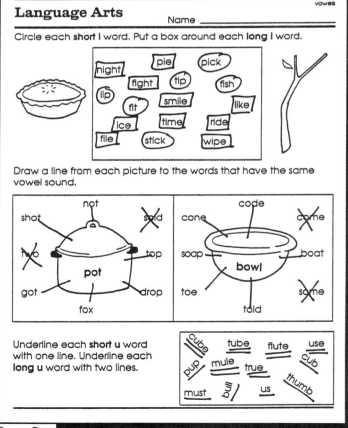

night   pie   pick
fight   tip   fish
lip
fit   smile   like
ice   time   ride
file   stick   wipe

Draw a line from each picture to the words that have the same vowel sound.

shot   not   sad
two   top
pot
got   drop
fox

cone   code   come
soap   boat
bowl
toe   some
told

Underline each **short u** word with one line. Underline each **long u** word with two lines.

cube   tube   flute   use
pup   mule   true   cub
must   bull   us   thumb

Page 7

Language Arts

Name _____

If the words on a pair of socks rhyme, color the socks. If they do not, put an **X** on the socks.

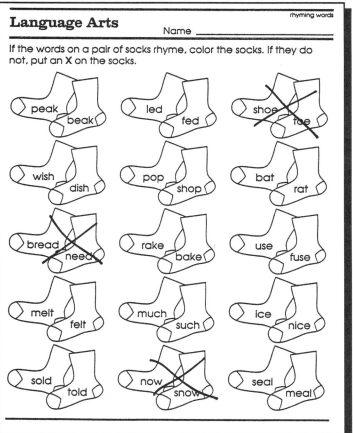

Page 8

Language Arts

Name _____

Synonyms are words that mean nearly the same thing. **Gift** and **present** are synonyms.

Look at the picture below. If a pair of words are **synonyms**, color the space **red**. If they are not, color the space **green**.

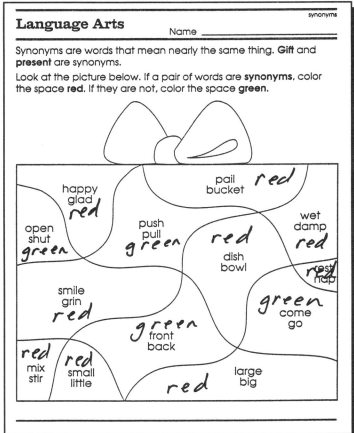

Page 9

Language Arts

Name _____

Find a word from the Word Box that is the **opposite** of the word on a bubble.

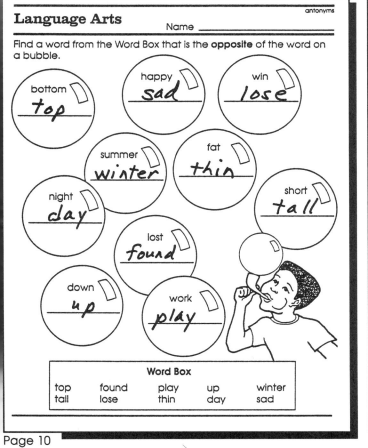

Word Box				
top	found	play	up	winter
tall	lose	thin	day	sad

Page 10

Language Arts

Name _____

Write a word from the Word Box to complete each sentence correctly.

1. **Wing** is to **bird** as **fin** is to ___fish___
2. **Boat** is to **ship** as **stone** is to ___rock___.
3. **Hive** is to **bee** as **barn** is to ___cow___
4. **Give** is to **take** as **hot** is to ___cold___
5. **Toe** is to **foot** as **finger** is to ___hand___.
6. **Coat** is to **jacket** as **smile** is to ___grin___.
7. **Snow** is to **snowy** as **sun** is to ___sunny___
8. **Come** is to **go** as **start** is to ___stop___
9. **Take** is to **took** as **see** is to ___saw___
10. **Tap** is to **tape** as **hat** is to ___hate___

Word Box				
cold	cow	fish	grin	hand
hate	rock	saw	stop	sunny

Page 11

Language Arts
classifying

Name _____

Put an **X** on the word in each list that does not belong. Write a word from the Word Box that does belong in the list.

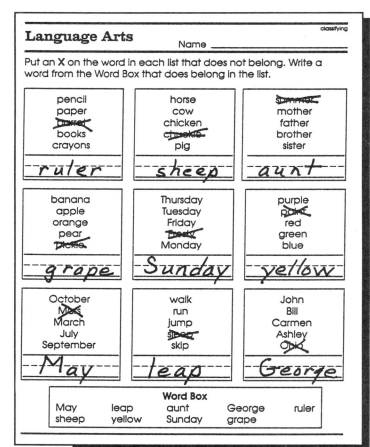

pencil paper ~~carrot~~ books crayons	horse cow chicken ~~cookie~~ pig	~~summer~~ mother father brother sister
ruler	_sheep_	_aunt_
banana apple orange pear ~~pickle~~	Thursday Tuesday Friday ~~treat~~ Monday	~~paint~~ red green blue
grape	_Sunday_	_yellow_
October ~~Max~~ March July September	walk run jump ~~stop~~ skip	John Bill Carmen Ashley ~~Oak~~
May	_leap_	_George_

Word Box

May	leap	aunt	George	ruler
sheep	yellow	Sunday	grape	

Language Arts
sequencing

Name _____

Number the pictures in the correct order.

2   1   4   3

Read the story.

Joel got his backpack. He opened it and took out his spelling book. Joel went to his desk. He wrote his spelling words two times each.

Underline which happened **first**.
a. Joel went to his desk.
b. Joel took out his book.

Underline which happened **last**.
a. Joel wrote his spelling words.
b. Joel opened his backpack.

Number the sentences in the correct order.
3 Kate cut out many shapes.
1 Kate mixed the dough.
4 Kate put the cookies on the cookie sheet.
2 She rolled out the dough.
5 She baked the cookies.

Language Arts
context clues

Name _____

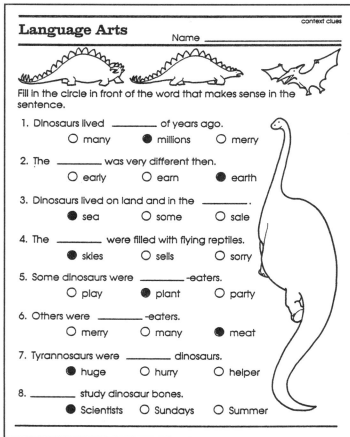

Fill in the circle in front of the word that makes sense in the sentence.

1. Dinosaurs lived _____ of years ago.
   ○ many   ● millions   ○ merry

2. The _____ was very different then.
   ○ early   ○ earn   ● earth

3. Dinosaurs lived on land and in the _____.
   ● sea   ○ some   ○ sale

4. The _____ were filled with flying reptiles.
   ● skies   ○ sells   ○ sorry

5. Some dinosaurs were _____-eaters.
   ○ play   ● plant   ○ party

6. Others were _____-eaters.
   ○ merry   ○ many   ● meat

7. Tyrannosaurs were _____ dinosaurs.
   ● huge   ○ hurry   ○ helper

8. _____ study dinosaur bones.
   ● Scientists   ○ Sundays   ○ Summer

Language Arts
cause and effect

Name _____

Draw a line from each **effect** to its **cause** to make a complete sentence.

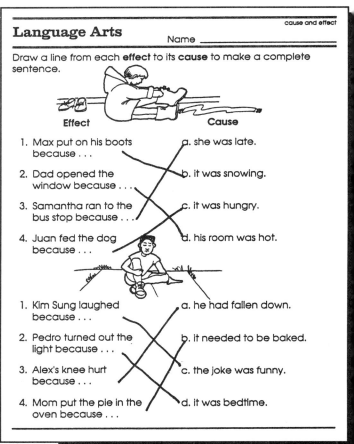

Effect   **Cause**

1. Max put on his boots because . . .   a. she was late.

2. Dad opened the window because . . .   b. it was snowing.

3. Samantha ran to the bus stop because . . . c. it was hungry.

4. Juan fed the dog because . . .   d. his room was hot.

1. Kim Sung laughed because . . .   a. he had fallen down.

2. Pedro turned out the light because . . . b. it needed to be baked.

3. Alex's knee hurt because . . .   c. the joke was funny.

4. Mom put the pie in the oven because . . . d. it was bedtime.

Language Arts
Name _____

Read each story carefully. Circle the picture that answers the question.

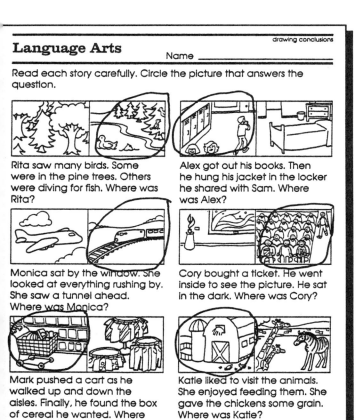

Rita saw many birds. Some were in the pine trees. Others were diving for fish. Where was Rita?

Alex got out his books. Then he hung his jacket in the locker he shared with Sam. Where was Alex?

Monica sat by the window. She looked at everything rushing by. She saw a tunnel ahead. Where was Monica?

Cory bought a ticket. He went inside to see the picture. He sat in the dark. Where was Cory?

Mark pushed a cart as he walked up and down the aisles. Finally, he found the box of cereal he wanted. Where was Mark?

Katie liked to visit the animals. She enjoyed feeding them. She gave the chickens some grain. Where was Katie?

Page 16

Language Arts
Name _____

Read each story. Underline the answer.

Sheri put her book aside. She pulled up the covers. She turned out the light.

What will Sheri do next?
a. read her book
b. go to sleep

Marvin stood in line. He got a tray of food. Marvin paid for his meal.

What will Marvin do next?
a. watch a movie
b. eat lunch

The doors opened. People got off. Chelsea got on. The doors closed.

What will Chelsea do next?
a. ride the bus
b. start to cry

Dale heard the siren. He saw the flashing lights. He heard the roar of the truck.

What will Dale do next?
a. call the fire station
b. get out of the way

Rita put on a life jacket. She stepped aboard. She saw the sails fill with wind.

What will Rita do next?
a. ride on a sailboat
b. swim in a swimming pool

Page 17

Language Arts
Name _____

In each story, underline the main idea sentence. Then, write one detail sentence on the lines below.

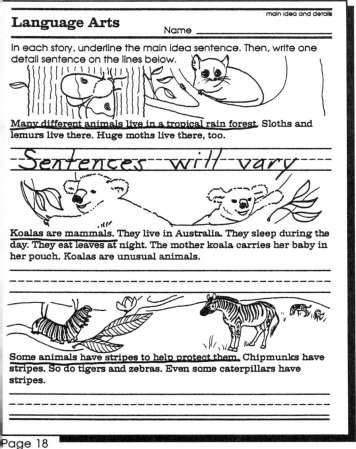

Many different animals live in a tropical rain forest. Sloths and lemurs live there. Huge moths live there, too.

Sentences will vary

Koalas are mammals. They live in Australia. They sleep during the day. They eat leaves at night. The mother koala carries her baby in her pouch. Koalas are unusual animals.

Some animals have stripes to help protect them. Chipmunks have stripes. So do tigers and zebras. Even some caterpillars have stripes.

Page 18

Language Arts
Name _____

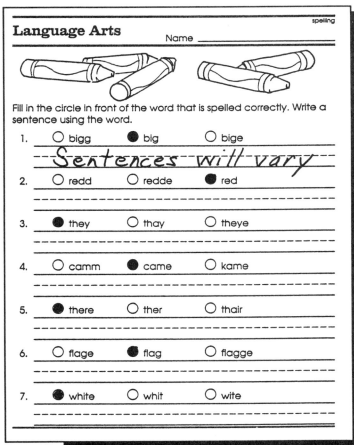

Fill in the circle in front of the word that is spelled correctly. Write a sentence using the word.

1. ○ bigg   ● big   ○ bige

Sentences will vary

2. ○ redd   ○ redde   ● red

3. ● they   ○ thay   ○ theye

4. ○ camm   ● came   ○ kame

5. ● there   ○ ther   ○ thair

6. ○ flage   ● flag   ○ flagge

7. ● white   ○ whit   ○ wite

Page 19

Page 20

Language Arts
Name _____

A **noun** is a word that names a **person, place,** or **thing.**
Use the code to color the spaces.

person—**red**   place—**blue**   thing—**green**

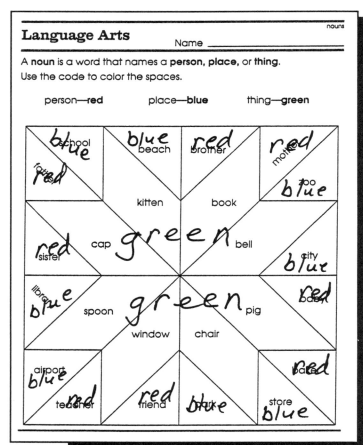

blue — school
blue — beach
red — brother
red — mother
red — (top)
blue — too
red — (top left)
kitten
book
red — cap
green
bell
red — sister
blue — city
blue — library
green
red — (dog)
blue — spoon
window
pig
chair
blue — airport
red — teacher
red — friend
blue
blue — store
red — (top right)

Page 20

Page 21

Language Arts
Name _____

A **pronoun** is a word that can take the place of a noun in a sentence. Circle the word that can take the place of the underlined word(s) in each sentence.

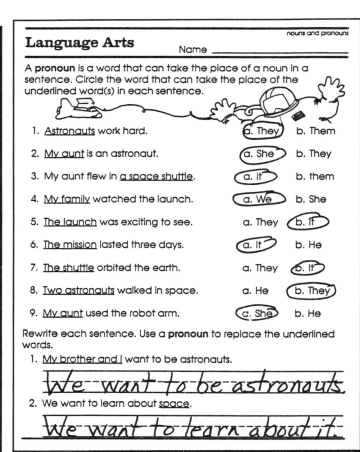

1. Astronauts work hard.   **a. They**   b. Them
2. My aunt is an astronaut.   **a. She**   b. They
3. My aunt flew in a space shuttle.   **a. it**   b. them
4. My family watched the launch.   **a. We**   b. She
5. The launch was exciting to see.   a. They   **b. It**
6. The mission lasted three days.   **a. It**   b. He
7. The shuttle orbited the earth.   a. They   **b. It**
8. Two astronauts walked in space.   a. He   **b. They**
9. My aunt used the robot arm.   **a. She**   b. He

Rewrite each sentence. Use a **pronoun** to replace the underlined words.

1. My brother and I want to be astronauts.

We want to be astronauts.

2. We want to learn about space.

We want to learn about it.

Page 21

Page 22

Language Arts
Name _____

A **word referent** sometimes takes the place of another word. Read each story. Fill in the circle in front of the correct answer to show what the underlined word stands for.

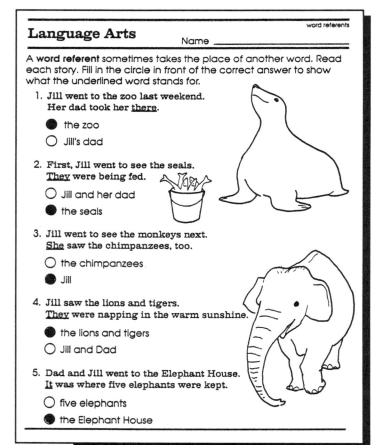

1. Jill went to the zoo last weekend.
   Her dad took her <u>there</u>.
   ● the zoo
   ○ Jill's dad

2. First, Jill went to see the seals.
   <u>They</u> were being fed.
   ○ Jill and her dad
   ● the seals

3. Jill went to see the monkeys next.
   <u>She</u> saw the chimpanzees, too.
   ○ the chimpanzees
   ● Jill

4. Jill saw the lions and tigers.
   <u>They</u> were napping in the warm sunshine.
   ● the lions and tigers
   ○ Jill and Dad

5. Dad and Jill went to the Elephant House.
   <u>It</u> was where five elephants were kept.
   ○ five elephants
   ● the Elephant House

Page 22

Page 23

Language Arts
Name _____

A **plural noun** names more than one person, place, or thing. Add an **s** to make most nouns plural. Circle the word that tells about the picture.

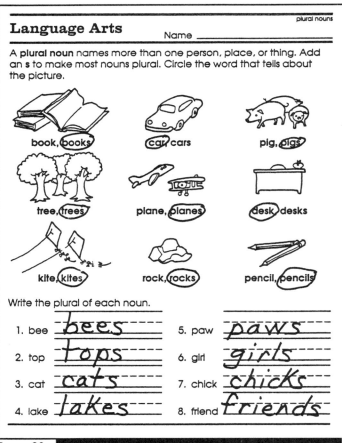

book, **books**   car, **cars**   pig, **pigs**

tree, **trees**   plane, **planes**   desk, **desks**

kite, **kites**   rock, **rocks**   pencil, **pencils**

Write the plural of each noun.

1. bee   _bees_   5. paw   _paws_
2. top   _tops_   6. girl   _girls_
3. cat   _cats_   7. chick _chicks_
4. lake   _lakes_   8. friend _friends_

Page 23

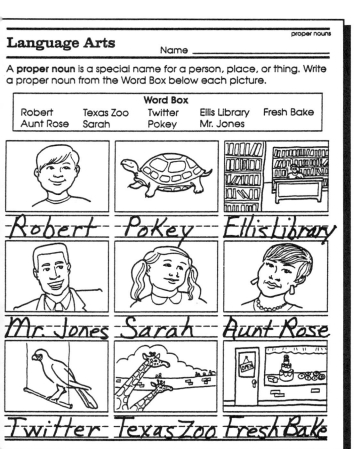

Language Arts

Name _____

A **proper noun** is a special name for a person, place, or thing. Write a proper noun from the Word Box below each picture.

Word Box

Robert	Texas Zoo	Twitter	Ellis Library	Fresh Bake
Aunt Rose	Sarah	Pokey	Mr. Jones	

Robert   Pokey   Ellis Library

Mr. Jones   Sarah   Aunt Rose

Twitter   Texas Zoo   Fresh Bake

Page 24

Language Arts

Name _____

A **verb** is an action word. Complete each sentence with the correct verb.

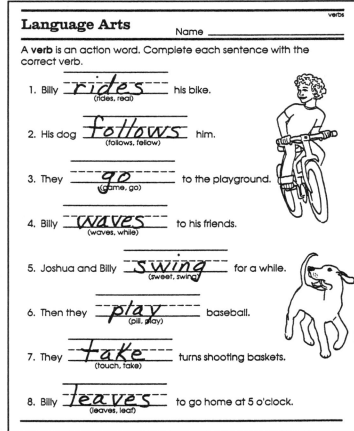

1. Billy _rides_ his bike.
   (rides, real)

2. His dog _follows_ him.
   (follows, fellow)

3. They _go_ to the playground.
   (game, go)

4. Billy _waves_ to his friends.
   (waves, while)

5. Joshua and Billy _swing_ for a while.
   (sweet, swing)

6. Then they _play_ baseball.
   (pill, play)

7. They _take_ turns shooting baskets.
   (touch, take)

8. Billy _leaves_ to go home at 5 o'clock.
   (leaves, leaf)

Page 25

Language Arts

Name _____

A **present tense verb** tells about action that is happening now.

Choose a present tense verb from the Word Box to complete each sentence.

Word Box

chases	barks	calls
gets	climbs	runs

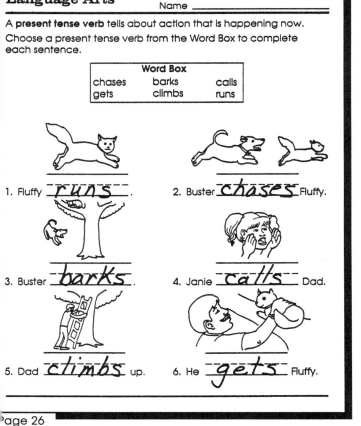

1. Fluffy _runs_ .

2. Buster _chases_ Fluffy.

3. Buster _barks_ .

4. Janie _calls_ Dad.

5. Dad _climbs_ up.

6. He _gets_ Fluffy.

Page 26

Language Arts

Name _____

A **past tense verb** tells about action that has already happened. Add **-ed** to most verbs to show the past tense. If the verb tells about action that has already happened, color the picture. If it does not, put an **X** on the picture.

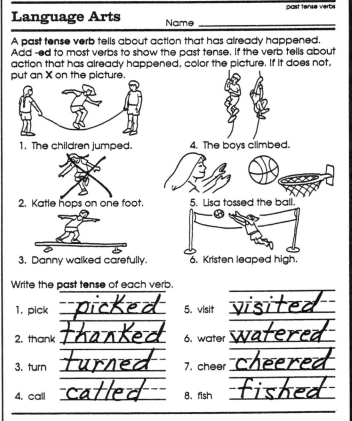

1. The children jumped.

2. Katie hops on one foot.

3. Danny walked carefully.

4. The boys climbed.

5. Lisa tossed the ball.

6. Kristen leaped high.

Write the **past tense** of each verb.

1. pick _picked_
2. thank _thanked_
3. turn _turned_
4. call _called_
5. visit _visited_
6. water _watered_
7. cheer _cheered_
8. fish _fished_

Page 27

A verb that does not show past tense by adding **-ed** is called an **irregular verb**. Complete each sentence with the correct verb.

1. Marta _made_ her own lunch for school yesterday.
   (makes, made)

2. First, she _got_ the bread.
   (gets, got)

3. Then she _spread_ on peanut butter.
   (spreads, spread)

4. Marta _took_ out the jelly.
   (took, takes)

5. She _put_ some jelly on the bread.
   (puts, put)

6. She also _found_ some potato chips to take.
   (found, finds)

Number the pictures in the correct order.

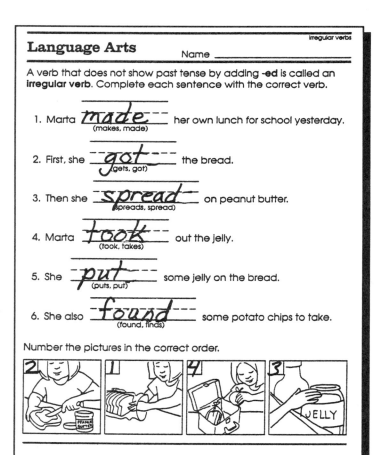

Page 28

A verb that does not show past tense by adding **-ed** is called an **irregular verb**. Complete each sentence with the correct **past tense** verb. _____

1. Our class _wrote_ a play.
   (writes, wrote)

2. We _gave_ it for our parents.
   (gave, give)

3. We _drew_ scenery for the play.
   (drew, draw)

4. Everyone _wore_ costumes.
   (wears, wore)

5. I _sang_ a song in the play.
   (sing, sang)

6. We _sold_ tickets to the play.
   (sold, sell)

7. We _made_ lemonade to sell, too.
   (make, made)

8. Many people _came_ to see our play.
   (come, came)

9. My dad _took_ a lot of pictures.
   (takes, took)

Page 29

Use **is** and **are** to tell about something that is happening **now**. Use **is** with one person, place, or thing. Use **are** with more than one.

Write **is** or **are** in each blank. Draw a picture in the box to tell about the story.

1. It _is_ cold today.

2. The winds _are_ strong.

3. The clouds _are_ gray.

4. The snow _is_ deep.

Pictures will vary.

Use **was** and **were** to tell about the **past**. Use **was** with one person, place, or thing. Use **were** with more than one.

1. Summer _was_ hot last year.

2. The sunshine _was_ bright.

3. My brother and I _were_ happy to go swimming.

4. The water _was_ cool.

Page 30

Add **-s** to a verb that tells what one person, animal, or thing does. Do not add **-s** to verbs that tell what two or more people, animals, or things do.

Write the correct verb.

1. Teddy _wants_ to go to the pet store.
   (want, wants)

2. He _asks_ Mom to take him.
   (ask, asks)

3. Mom and Teddy _get_ into the car.
   (get, gets)

4. They _drive_ to the mall.
   (drive, drives)

5. Teddy _runs_ ahead to the store.
   (run, runs)

6. He _sees_ just what he wants.
   (see, sees)

7. A puppy with sad eyes _looks_ up at Teddy.
   (look, looks)

8. Teddy _hugs_ the little dog.
   (hug, hugs)

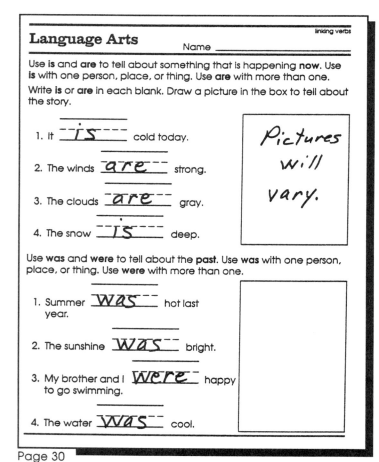

Page 31

Page 32

Language Arts
Name _____

An **adjective** describes or tells about a noun. Number words and color words are adjectives.

Color the spaces with number words yellow. Color the spaces with color words green. If the word is not an adjective, color the space blue.

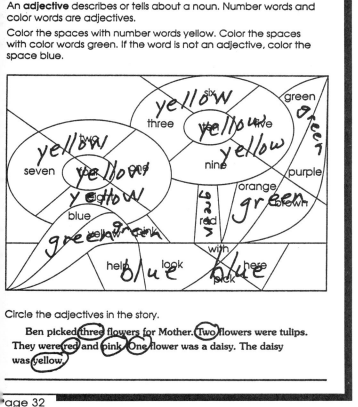

Circle the adjectives in the story.

Ben picked three flowers for Mother. Two flowers were tulips. They were red and pink. One flower was a daisy. The daisy was yellow.

Page 33

Language Arts
Name _____

An **adjective** describes or tells about a noun. Choose an adjective from the Word Box to describe each noun pictured below.

Word Box		
tiny	fuzzy	large
long	curly	short

1. a _long_ tail
2. _short_ ears
3. a _fuzzy_ chick
4. a _curly_ tail
5. the _large_ cow
6. the _tiny_ mouse

Circle the adjective in each phrase. Underline the noun it describes.

1. the soft kitten
2. the little duckling
3. the funny goat
4. a loud rooster
5. the lovely swan
6. the strong ox

Page 34

Language Arts
Name _____

Add **-er** to most **adjectives** to compare two things. Add **-est** to most **adjectives** to compare more than two things.

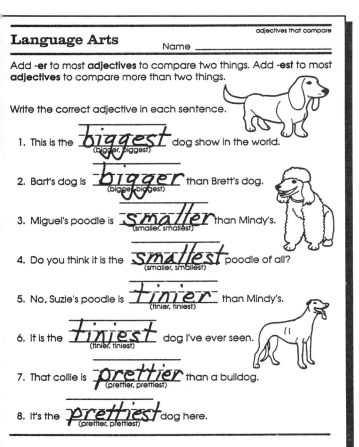

Write the correct adjective in each sentence.

1. This is the _biggest_ dog show in the world.
   (bigger, biggest)
2. Bart's dog is _bigger_ than Brett's dog.
   (bigger, biggest)
3. Miguel's poodle is _smaller_ than Mindy's.
   (smaller, smallest)
4. Do you think it is the _smallest_ poodle of all?
   (smaller, smallest)
5. No, Suzie's poodle is _tinier_ than Mindy's.
   (tinier, tiniest)
6. It is the _tiniest_ dog I've ever seen.
   (tinier, tiniest)
7. That collie is _prettier_ than a bulldog.
   (prettier, prettiest)
8. It's the _prettiest_ dog here.
   (prettier, prettiest)

Page 35

Language Arts
Name _____

A **sentence** is a group of words that tells a complete idea.

Write **S** on the bear if the group of words makes a sentence. Draw an **X** on the bear if it does not.

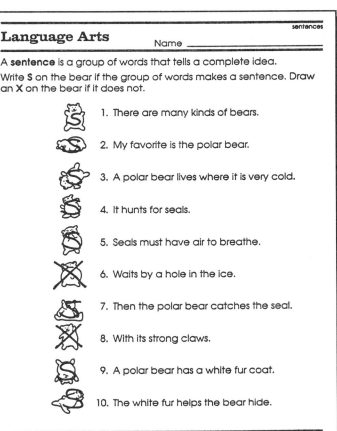

1. There are many kinds of bears.
2. My favorite is the polar bear.
3. A polar bear lives where it is very cold.
4. It hunts for seals.
5. Seals must have air to breathe.
6. Waits by a hole in the ice.
7. Then the polar bear catches the seal.
8. With its strong claws.
9. A polar bear has a white fur coat.
10. The white fur helps the bear hide.

Language Arts

Name _____

The **subject** of a sentence tells who or what does something.
Underline the subject of each sentence.

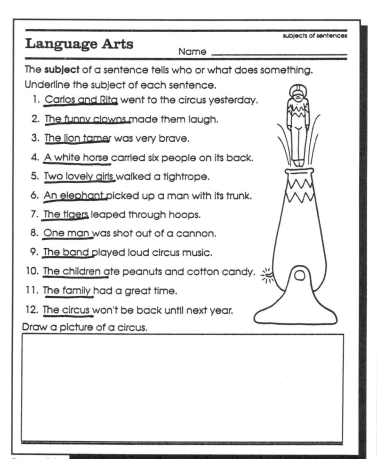

1. <u>Carlos and Rita</u> went to the circus yesterday.
2. <u>The funny clowns</u> made them laugh.
3. <u>The lion tamer</u> was very brave.
4. <u>A white horse</u> carried six people on its back.
5. <u>Two lovely girls</u> walked a tightrope.
6. <u>An elephant</u> picked up a man with its trunk.
7. <u>The tigers</u> leaped through hoops.
8. <u>One man</u> was shot out of a cannon.
9. <u>The band</u> played loud circus music.
10. <u>The children</u> ate peanuts and cotton candy.
11. <u>The family</u> had a great time.
12. <u>The circus</u> won't be back until next year.

Draw a picture of a circus.

Page 36

Language Arts

Name _____

The **predicate** of a sentence tells what the subject **is** or **does**.
Underline the predicate of the sentence with two lines.

1. My family <u>helps save the earth.</u>
2. We <u>recycle aluminum cans.</u>
3. I <u>smash the cans for Dad.</u>
4. We <u>try not to use much paper.</u>
5. My mother <u>cleans with rags.</u>
6. I <u>use both sides of a sheet of paper.</u>
7. I <u>take a lunch box to school instead of a paper sack.</u>
8. We <u>collect old newspapers to recycle.</u>
9. The family <u>is careful with water.</u>
10. We <u>shower instead of taking a bath.</u>
11. Dad <u>fixes leaky faucets.</u>
12. We <u>turn out lights when we can.</u>

Write a sentence to tell what you can do to save the environment.

Sentences will vary.

Page 37

Language Arts

Name _____

A **statement** is a sentence that tells something. It begins with a **capital letter** and ends with a period. Write each sentence correctly.

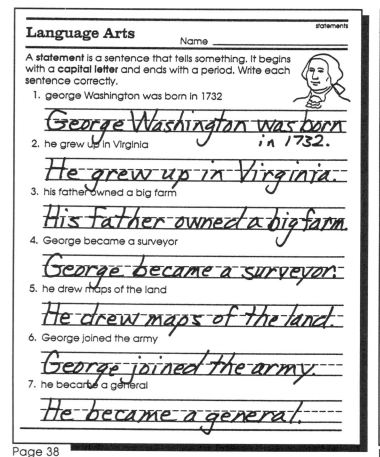

1. george Washington was born in 1732

George Washington was born in 1732.

2. he grew up in Virginia

He grew up in Virginia.

3. his father owned a big farm

His father owned a big farm.

4. George became a surveyor

George became a surveyor.

5. he drew maps of the land

He drew maps of the land.

6. George joined the army

George joined the army.

7. he became a general

He became a general.

Page 38

Language Arts

Name _____

A **question** is a sentence that asks something. It begins with a **capital letter** and ends with a **question mark**.

If the sentence asks a question, add a question mark and color the top hat black. If it does not ask a question, draw an **X** on the top hat.

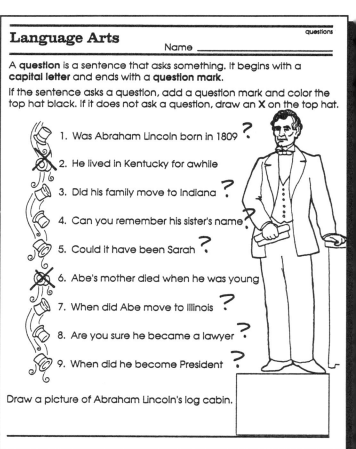

1. Was Abraham Lincoln born in 1809 **?**
2. He lived in Kentucky for awhile
3. Did his family move to Indiana **?**
4. Can you remember his sister's name **?**
5. Could it have been Sarah **?**
6. Abe's mother died when he was young
7. When did Abe move to Illinois **?**
8. Are you sure he became a lawyer **?**
9. When did he become President **?**

Draw a picture of Abraham Lincoln's log cabin.

Page 39

A **statement** is a sentence that tells something. A **question** is a sentence that asks something.

Change the word order to make each statement into a question and make each question into a statement. Write the new sentence on the line. Remember to begin each sentence with a capital letter and use the correct end mark.

1. Have you read about Pecos Bill?

You have read about Pecos Bill.

2. "Pecos Bill" is a tall tale.

Is "Pecos Bill" a tall tale?

3. Bill did get lost from his parents.

Did Bill get lost from his parents?

4. Was Bill raised by coyotes?

Bill was raised by coyotes.

5. Did Bill think he was a coyote?

Bill did think he was a coyote.

6. Bill was told he was a Texan.

Was Bill told he was a Texan?

A special name for a person or a pet begins with a **capital letter**. Write each name correctly on the line.

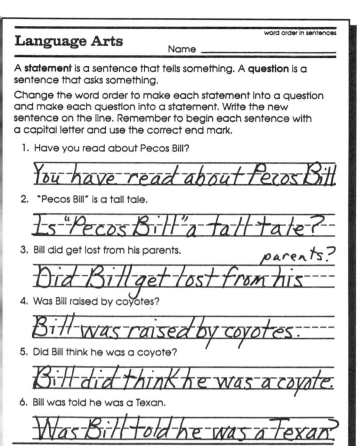

jane — 1. *Jane*

steven — 4. *Steven*

fluffy — 2. *Fluffy*

erica — 5. *Erica*

pete — 3. *Pete*

buster — 6. *Buster*

Fill in the circle below the word if the word should begin with a capital letter.

1. Yesterday judy and I took our dog to the vet.

2. We saw suzie there with her cat, muffin.

3. The kitten and sparky chased each other.

Begin a person's **first**, **middle**, and **last name** with a **capital letter**. An **initial** also begins with a capital letter. Write each name correctly.

sue ann lewis
1. *Sue Ann Lewis*

billy buford
5. *Billy Buford*

emily jeffers
2. *Emily Jeffers*

mike lopez
6. *Mike Lopez*

juan mendoza
3. *Juan Mendoza*

kim lee tran
7. *Kim Lee Tran*

barry w. churchill
4. *Barry W. Churchill*

carol kruger
Carol Kruger

Begin titles such as **Mr., Mrs., Ms.** and **Miss** with **capital letters**. Write each name correctly.

mr. george jones
1. *Mr. George Jones*

ms. j. r. treadwell
3. *Ms. J. R. Treadwell*

miss mary smith
2. *Miss Mary Smith*

mr. and mrs. carlson
4. *Mr. and Mrs. Carlson*

The name of a **special place** begins with a **capital letter**. Write the name of each special place correctly. Use the Word Box.

Word Box

city hall	forest park	green's market
buder school	game land	modern museum
oakland station	denver zoo	

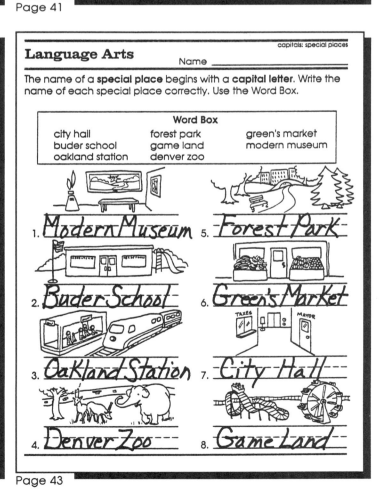

1. *Modern Museum*

5. *Forest Park*

2. *Buder School*

6. *Green's Market*

3. *Oakland Station*

7. *City Hall*

4. *Denver Zoo*

8. *Game Land*

Language Arts

Name _____

Begin the name of a street with a capital letter. If the word street, road, drive, court, or avenue is used with the street's name, capitalize it also. **Examples:** Market Street, Berry Road

Write the street names correctly.

1. turner avenue — *Turner Avenue*
2. appleton court — *Appleton Court*
3. drexel drive — *Drexel Drive*
4. tenth street — *Tenth Street*
5. forest road — *Forest Road*

The name of a state begins with a capital letter. Write the names correctly.

1. alaska — *Alaska*   4. florida — *Florida*
2. maine — *Marne*   5. oregon — *Oregon*
3. kentucky — *Kentucky*   6. wyoming — *Wyoming*

Write the name of your state. *Answers will vary.*

Page 44

Language Arts

Name _____

The name of each **day** of the week and **month** of the year begins with a **capital letter**.

Write each day and month correctly.

1. wednesday — *Wednesday*
2. february — *February*
3. sunday — *Sunday*
4. august — *August*
5. saturday — *Saturday*
6. april — *April*
7. tuesday — *Tuesday*

Names for **special days** and **holidays** begin with **capital letters**. Fill in the circle of the correctly written special day or holiday.

1. ○ christmas eve   4. ○ Independence day
   ● Christmas Eve   ● Independence Day

2. ○ Groundhog day   5. ● Mother's Day
   ● Groundhog Day   ○ mother's Day

3. ● Hanukkah   6. ● Thanksgiving
   ○ hanukkah   ○ thanksgiving

Page 45

Language Arts

Name _____

Use a **period** at the end of a **statement** or after an **abbreviation**.

Write the word or initial that should be followed by a period. Add the period.

1. Mr Hall came to visit my classroom. — *Mr.*
2. They came to talk about our city — *city.*
3. I live in St Louis. — *St.*
4. Some streets were named for famous people — *people.*
5. One was named for Charles A. Lindbergh — *Lindbergh*

Write the abbreviation for each word. Use the Word Box.

Word Box			
Dr.	Mr.	Sept.	Mon.
Nov.	Rd.	Ave.	St.

1. Mister — *Mr.*   5. Doctor — *Dr.*
2. Street — *St.*   6. Road — *Rd.*
3. Monday — *Mon.*   7. September — *Sept.*
4. Avenue — *Ave.*   8. November — *Nov.*

Page 46

Language Arts

Name _____

Use a **question mark** after a sentence that asks a question. If the sentence asks a question, color the tooth and add the question mark. If it does not, draw an **X** on the tooth.

1. Have you ever been to the dentist ?
2. Were you afraid to go ?
3. Do you brush your teeth twice a day ?
4. Can you use floss correctly ?
5. The dentist can show you how
6. Did you have any cavities ?
7. I go to the dentist twice a year

Write each question correctly.

1. Have you lost any teeth — *Have you lost any teeth?*
2. How many have you lost — *How many have you lost?*
3. Can you name the back teeth — *Can you name the back teeth?*

Page 47

Language Arts

Name _____

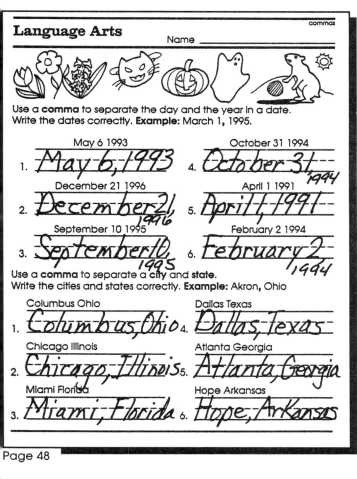

Use a **comma** to separate the day and the year in a date.
Write the dates correctly. **Example:** March 1, 1995.

May 6 1993
1. *May 6, 1993*

October 31 1994
4. *October 31, 1994*

December 21 1996
2. *December 21, 1996*

April 1 1991
5. *April 1, 1991*

September 10 1995
3. *September 10, 1995*

February 2 1994
6. *February 2, 1994*

Use a **comma** to separate a **city** and **state**.
Write the cities and states correctly. **Example:** Akron, Ohio

Columbus Ohio
1. *Columbus, Ohio*

Dallas Texas
4. *Dallas, Texas*

Chicago Illinois
2. *Chicago, Illinois*

Atlanta Georgia
5. *Atlanta, Georgia*

Miami Florida
3. *Miami, Florida*

Hope Arkansas
6. *Hope, Arkansas*

Page 48

Language Arts

Name _____

A friendly letter has a **date**, **greeting**, **body**, **closing**, and **signature**.

> **(date)** → March 7, 1995
>
> Dear Aunt Molly, ← **(greeting)**
> **(body)** → { Thank you for inviting me to meet you in Topeka. I will be happy to see you again.
>
> Love, ← **(closing)**
> Megan ← **(signature)**

Copy the letter correctly on these lines.

March 7, 1995
Dear Aunt Molly,
Thank you for inviting me
to meet you in Topeka. I will be
happy to see you again. Love,
Megan

1. What is the date on the letter? *March 7, 1995*

2. Who wrote the letter? *Megan*

Page 49

Language Arts

Name _____

A **paragraph** has a sentence that tells the **main idea**. All the other sentences in a paragraph must tell about the main idea.

Read the paragraph. Draw a line through the sentence that does not tell about the main idea.

> Unusual plants and animals live in the desert. Hairy tarantulas live there. ~~My family drove through the desert.~~ Saguaro cactuses grow in the desert.

A paragraph is written in a special form. The first sentence is **indented**. The other sentences follow each other. Write the sentences below in **paragraph form**. Leave out the sentence that does not tell about the main idea.

Pandas are interesting animals.
They are not bears.
They belong to the raccoon family.
Pandas live in China.

They have woolly black and white fur.
People in China eat rice.
Bamboo shoots are their favorite food.

Pandas are interesting animals. They are not bears. They belong to the raccoon family. Pandas live in China. They have woolly black and white fur. Bamboo shoots are their favorite food.

Page 50

Language Arts

Name _____

Fill in this form to tell about a book you have read.

Book Title: *Answers will vary.*

Author: _____

Illustrator: _____

Check one. This book was: **fiction** _____ **non-fiction** _____ .

This book was mainly about _____

The part I liked best was _____

Write some new words from the book. _____

1. _____ 3. _____

2. _____ 4. _____

Circle one. This book was . . . **great** **okay** **terrible**

Page 51

Language Arts

Name _____

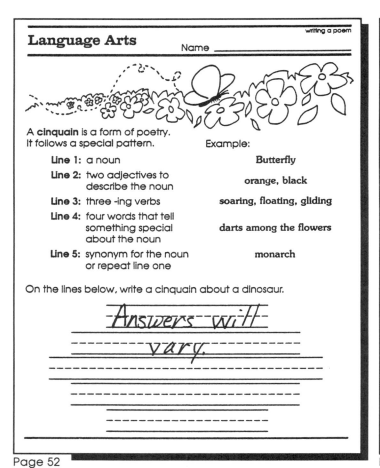

A **cinquain** is a form of poetry. It follows a special pattern.

Example:

Line 1: a noun

Line 2: two adjectives to describe the noun

Line 3: three -ing verbs

Line 4: four words that tell something special about the noun

Line 5: synonym for the noun or repeat line one

Butterfly

orange, black

soaring, floating, gliding

darts among the flowers

monarch

On the lines below, write a cinquain about a dinosaur.

Answers will vary.

Page 52

Language Arts

Name _____

Write the words in ABC order on the shapes.

good
crunchy
red
apple

apple
crunchy
good
red

kite
wind
tail
fly

fly
Kite
tail
wind

roof
door
window
house

door
house
roof
window

read
enjoy
book
words

book
enjoy
read
words

Page 53

Language Arts

Name _____

Answer the questions about this **Table of Contents**. A Table of Contents tells the chapters found in a book and the page each one starts on.

Table of Contents

Chapter	Page
The Sun	1
The Inner Planets	12
The Earth	18
Our Closest Neighbor	23
The Outer Planets	30

1. How many chapters are in the book?   *5*

2. Which chapter follows *The Inner Planets*?   *The Earth*

3. On which page does *The Earth* begin?   *18*

4. On which page does *The Outer Planets* begin?   *30*

5. On which page does *The Sun* end?   *11*

6. What is the title of the last chapter?

   The Outer Planets

7. What is the title of the third chapter?

   The Earth

8. What information is in a Table of Contents?

   chapters in a book and the page each one begins.

Page 54

Math

Name _____

Circle how many.

3 (4) 5

6 (7) 8

(5) 6 7

7 8 (9)

4 5 (6)

(0) 1 2

Write how many.

8

10

6

5

7

9

Write the missing numbers.

0 *1* *2* *3* 4 *5* 6 7 8 9 10

Page 55

Math

Name _____

Count a set of gum balls. Cut and paste it on the correct machine.

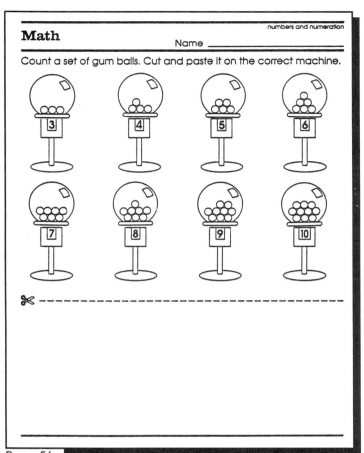

✂ -

Math

Name _____

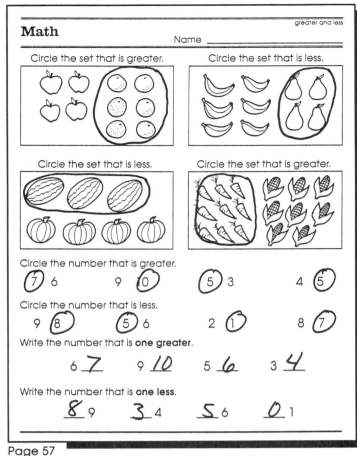

Circle the set that is greater.

Circle the set that is less.

Circle the set that is less.

Circle the set that is greater.

Circle the number that is greater.

7 6   9 10   5 3   4 5

Circle the number that is less.

9 8   5 6   2 1   8 7

Write the number that is **one greater**.

6 7   9 10   5 6   3 4

Write the number that is **one less**.

8 9   3 4   5 6   0 1

Math

Name _____

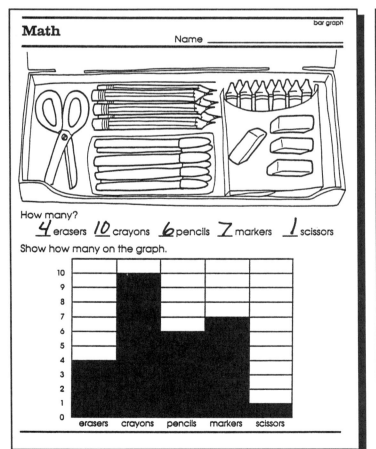

How many?

4 erasers 10 crayons 6 pencils 7 markers 1 scissors

Show how many on the graph.

Math

Name _____

Add. Color spaces with answers **less than** 5 red. Color spaces with answers of 5 blue. Color answers **greater than** 5 green.

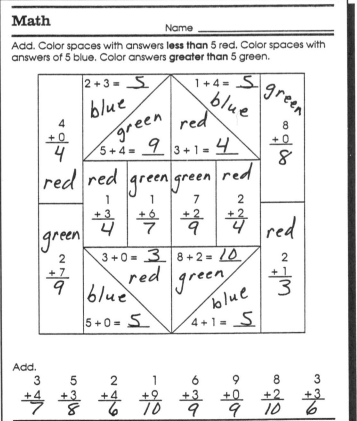

$2 + 3 = 5$ blue
$1 + 4 = 5$ blue
green

green red

$\begin{array}{r}4\\+0\\\hline4\end{array}$

$5 + 4 = 9$ green
$3 + 1 = 4$ red

$\begin{array}{r}8\\+0\\\hline8\end{array}$

red red green green red

$\begin{array}{r}1\\+3\\\hline4\end{array}$ $\begin{array}{r}1\\+6\\\hline7\end{array}$ $\begin{array}{r}7\\+2\\\hline9\end{array}$ $\begin{array}{r}2\\+2\\\hline4\end{array}$

green

red

$\begin{array}{r}2\\+7\\\hline9\end{array}$

$3 + 0 = 3$ red
$8 + 2 = 10$ green

$\begin{array}{r}2\\+1\\\hline3\end{array}$

blue
$5 + 0 = 5$
blue
$4 + 1 = 5$

Add.

$\begin{array}{r}3\\+4\\\hline7\end{array}$ $\begin{array}{r}5\\+3\\\hline8\end{array}$ $\begin{array}{r}2\\+4\\\hline6\end{array}$ $\begin{array}{r}1\\+9\\\hline10\end{array}$ $\begin{array}{r}6\\+3\\\hline9\end{array}$ $\begin{array}{r}9\\+0\\\hline9\end{array}$ $\begin{array}{r}8\\+2\\\hline10\end{array}$ $\begin{array}{r}3\\+3\\\hline6\end{array}$

117

Add. Color answers of **8 red, 9 blue,** and **10 brown.**

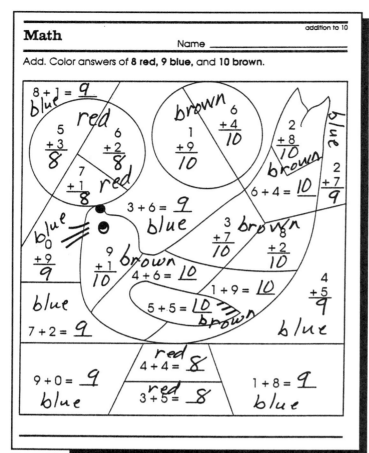

$8 + 1 = 9$ blue

red

$\begin{array}{r} 5 \\ +3 \\ \hline 8 \end{array}$ $\begin{array}{r} 6 \\ +2 \\ \hline 8 \end{array}$

$\begin{array}{r} 7 \\ +1 \\ \hline 8 \end{array}$ red

$3 + 6 = 9$ blue

brown $\begin{array}{r} 6 \\ +4 \\ \hline 10 \end{array}$

$\begin{array}{r} 1 \\ +9 \\ \hline 10 \end{array}$

$\begin{array}{r} 2 \\ +8 \\ \hline 10 \end{array}$ brown

$6 + 4 = 10$

$\begin{array}{r} 2 \\ +7 \\ \hline 9 \end{array}$ blue

$\begin{array}{r} 0 \\ +9 \\ \hline 9 \end{array}$ blue

$\begin{array}{r} 9 \\ +1 \\ \hline 10 \end{array}$ brown

$4 + 6 = 10$

$5 + 5 = 10$ brown

$\begin{array}{r} 3 \\ +7 \\ \hline 10 \end{array}$ brown

$\begin{array}{r} 8 \\ +2 \\ \hline 10 \end{array}$

$1 + 9 = 10$

$\begin{array}{r} 4 \\ +5 \\ \hline 9 \end{array}$ blue

$7 + 2 = 9$

$9 + 0 = 9$ blue

$4 + 4 = 8$ red

$3 + 5 = 8$ red

$1 + 8 = 9$ blue

Subtract.

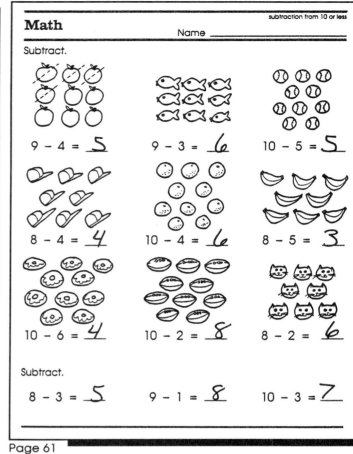

$9 - 4 = 5$ $9 - 3 = 6$ $10 - 5 = 5$

$8 - 4 = 4$ $10 - 4 = 6$ $8 - 5 = 3$

$10 - 6 = 4$ $10 - 2 = 8$ $8 - 2 = 6$

Subtract.

$8 - 3 = 5$ $9 - 1 = 8$ $10 - 3 = 7$

Write a subtraction problem for each picture.

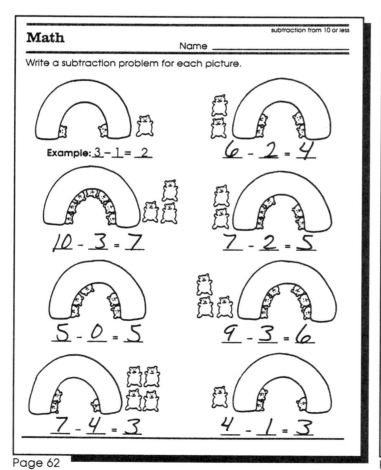

Example: $3 - 1 = 2$

$6 - 2 = 4$

$10 - 3 = 7$

$7 - 2 = 5$

$5 - 0 = 5$

$9 - 3 = 6$

$7 - 4 = 3$

$4 - 1 = 3$

Solve. Follow the code to color the picture.

2 — red   **3** — blue   **4** — yellow   **5** — brown   **6** — black

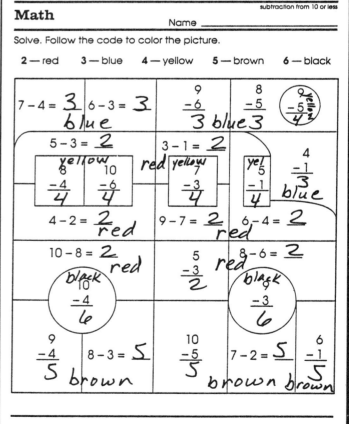

$7 - 4 = 3$ blue $6 - 3 = 3$ $\begin{array}{r} 9 \\ -6 \\ \hline 3 \end{array}$ blue $\begin{array}{r} 8 \\ -5 \\ \hline 3 \end{array}$ $\begin{array}{r} 9 \\ -5 \\ \hline 4 \end{array}$ yellow

$5 - 3 = 2$ yellow $\begin{array}{r} 8 \\ -4 \\ \hline 4 \end{array}$ $\begin{array}{r} 10 \\ -6 \\ \hline 4 \end{array}$ red $3 - 1 = 2$ yellow $\begin{array}{r} 7 \\ -3 \\ \hline 4 \end{array}$ $\begin{array}{r} 5 \\ -1 \\ \hline 4 \end{array}$ yel $\begin{array}{r} 4 \\ -1 \\ \hline 3 \end{array}$ blue

$4 - 2 = 2$ red $9 - 7 = 2$ red $6 - 4 = 2$

$10 - 8 = 2$ red $\begin{array}{r} 10 \\ -4 \\ \hline 6 \end{array}$ black $\begin{array}{r} 5 \\ -3 \\ \hline 2 \end{array}$ red $8 - 6 = 2$ $\begin{array}{r} 10 \\ -3 \\ \hline 6 \end{array}$ black

$\begin{array}{r} 9 \\ -4 \\ \hline 5 \end{array}$ brown $8 - 3 = 5$ $\begin{array}{r} 10 \\ -5 \\ \hline 5 \end{array}$ $7 - 2 = 5$ brown $\begin{array}{r} 6 \\ -1 \\ \hline 5 \end{array}$ brown

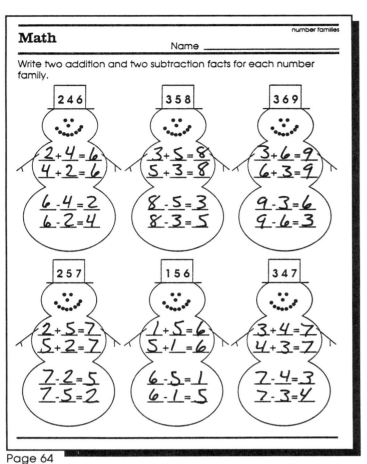

Math

Name _____

number families

Write two addition and two subtraction facts for each number family.

2 4 6
2 + 4 = 6
4 + 2 = 6
6 - 4 = 2
6 - 2 = 4

3 5 8
3 + 5 = 8
5 + 3 = 8
8 - 5 = 3
8 - 3 = 5

3 6 9
3 + 6 = 9
6 + 3 = 9
9 - 3 = 6
9 - 6 = 3

2 5 7
2 + 5 = 7
5 + 2 = 7
7 - 2 = 5
7 - 5 = 2

1 5 6
1 + 5 = 6
5 + 1 = 6
6 - 5 = 1
6 - 1 = 5

3 4 7
3 + 4 = 7
4 + 3 = 7
7 - 4 = 3
7 - 3 = 4

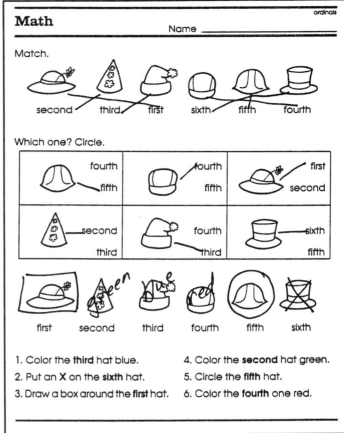

Math

Name _____

ordinals

Match.

second   third   first   sixth   fifth   fourth

Which one? Circle.

fourth — fifth   fourth — fifth   first — second

second — third   fourth — third   sixth — fifth

first   second   third   fourth   fifth   sixth

1. Color the **third** hat blue.
2. Put an **X** on the **sixth** hat.
3. Draw a box around the **first** hat.
4. Color the **second** hat green.
5. Circle the **fifth** hat.
6. Color the **fourth** one red.

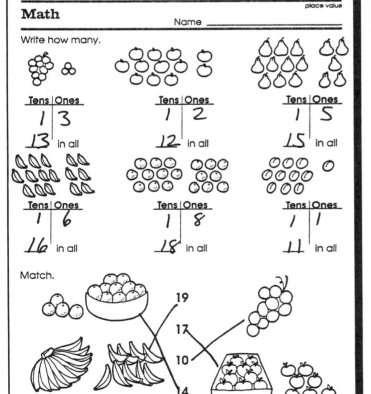

Math

Name _____

place value

Write how many.

Tens	Ones
1	3

13 in all

Tens	Ones
1	2

12 in all

Tens	Ones
1	5

15 in all

Tens	Ones
1	6

16 in all

Tens	Ones
1	8

18 in all

Tens	Ones
1	1

11 in all

Match.

19
17
10
14

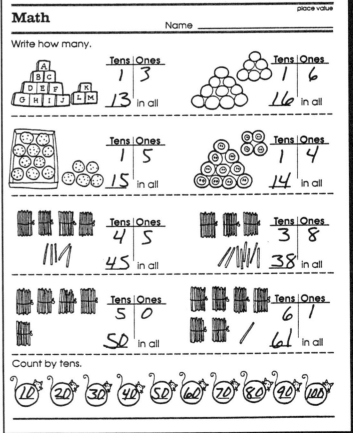

Math

Name _____

place value

Write how many.

Tens	Ones
1	3

13 in all

Tens	Ones
1	6

16 in all

Tens	Ones
1	5

15 in all

Tens	Ones
1	4

14 in all

Tens	Ones
4	5

45 in all

Tens	Ones
3	8

38 in all

Tens	Ones
5	0

50 in all

Tens	Ones
6	1

61 in all

Count by tens.

10 20 30 40 50 60 70 80 90 100

         IF8783 First Grade in Review

Page 68

Color balloons with numbers between **20** and **30** red.
Color balloons with numbers between **40** and **50** purple.
Color balloons with numbers between **60** and **70** blue.
Color balloons with numbers between **80** and **90** green.
Color all other balloons **yellow**.

Page 69

Write each time.

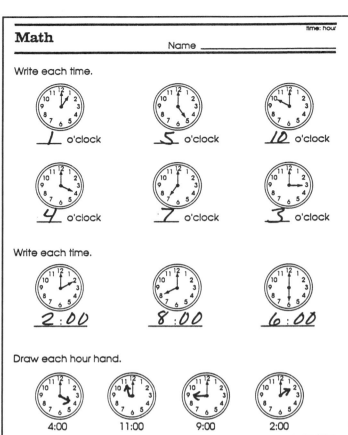

1 o'clock   5 o'clock   10 o'clock

4 o'clock   7 o'clock   3 o'clock

Write each time.

2:00   8:00   6:00

Draw each hour hand.

4:00   11:00   9:00   2:00

Page 70

Write each time.

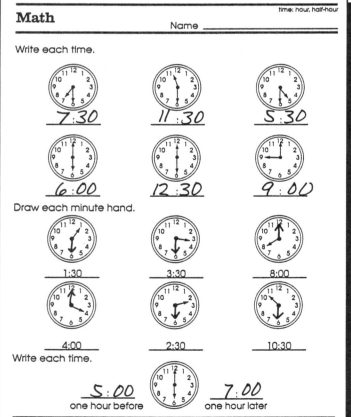

7:30   11:30   5:30

6:00   12:30   9:00

Draw each minute hand.

1:30   3:30   8:00

4:00   2:30   10:30

Write each time.

5:00   7:00
one hour before   one hour later

Page 71

Study the calendar and the key. Answer the questions.

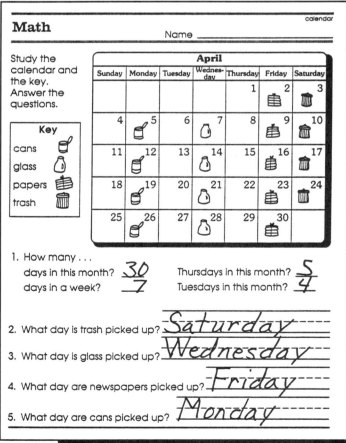

			April			
Sunday	Monday	Tuesday	Wednesday	Thursday	Friday	Saturday
					1	2	3

1. How many . . .
   days in this month? __30__   Thursdays in this month? __5__
   days in a week? __7__   Tuesdays in this month? __4__

2. What day is trash picked up? _Saturday_

3. What day is glass picked up? _Wednesday_

4. What day are newspapers picked up? _Friday_

5. What day are cans picked up? _Monday_

Page 72

Math

Name _____

money

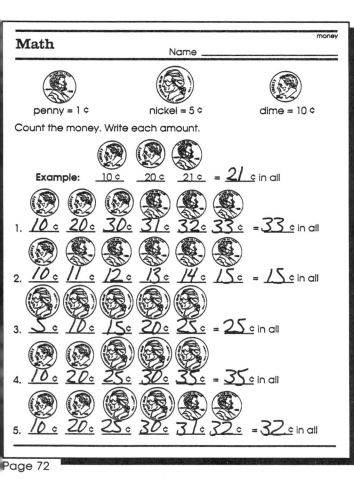

penny = 1 ¢   nickel = 5 ¢   dime = 10 ¢

Count the money. Write each amount.

Example: 10 ¢   20 ¢   21 ¢ = **21** ¢ in all

1. **10** ¢ **20** ¢ **30** ¢ **31** ¢ **32** ¢ **33** ¢ = **33** ¢ in all

2. **10** ¢ **11** ¢ **12** ¢ **13** ¢ **14** ¢ **15** ¢ = **15** ¢ in all

3. **5** ¢ **10** ¢ **15** ¢ **20** ¢ **25** ¢ = **25** ¢ in all

4. **10** ¢ **20** ¢ **25** ¢ **30** ¢ **35** ¢ = **35** ¢ in all

5. **10** ¢ **20** ¢ **25** ¢ **30** ¢ **31** ¢ **32** ¢ = **32** ¢ in all

Page 72

Page 73

Math

Name _____

money

Circle the coins needed to buy each item.

15¢

30¢

45¢

69¢

Write and solve the problem.

You have.	You find.	Total
		9 ¢ + **1** ¢ = **10** ¢
		11 ¢ + **5** ¢ = **16** ¢
		25 ¢ + **10** ¢ = **35** ¢
		30 ¢ + **20** ¢ = **50** ¢

Page 73

Page 74

Math

Name _____

problem solving: money

Solve the problems.

1. You had 10¢.
   You saved 7¢ more.
   How much do you have
   in all? **17** ¢

2. You had 8¢.
   You earned 6¢ more.
   How much do you have
   in all? **14** ¢

3. You have 15¢.
   You spent 6¢.
   How much is left? **9** ¢

4. You find 7¢.
   You earn 9¢ more.
   How much do you have
   in all? **16** ¢

5. 5¢
   How much is two? **10** ¢

6. You have 12¢.
   You buy 8¢
   How much is left **4** ¢

7. 8¢ 7¢
   How much for both? **15** ¢

8. You have
   You buy 9¢
   How much is left? **8** ¢

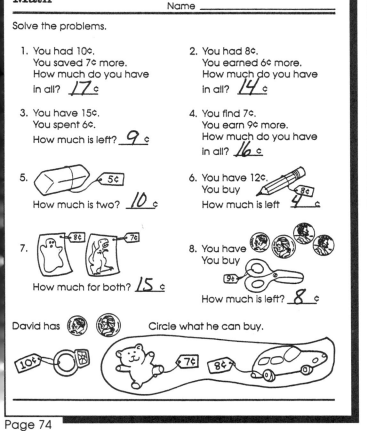

David has   Circle what he can buy.

10¢   7¢   8¢

Page 74

Page 75

Math

Name _____

measuring length

How long is each stick?

1. about **1**

2. about **3**

3. about **2**

4. about **4**

5. about **9** cm

6. about **7** cm

7. about **5** cm

8. about **4** inches

9. about **2** inches

10. about **3** inches

Page 75

Continue each pattern.

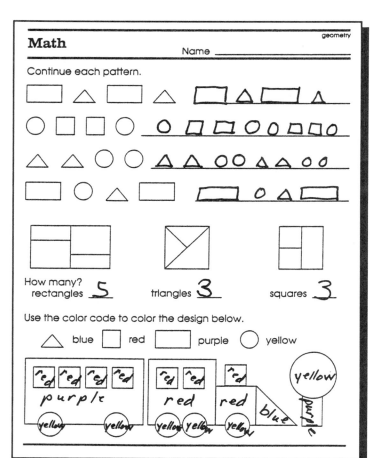

How many?
rectangles **5**   triangles **3**   squares **3**

Use the color code to color the design below.

△ blue   □ red   ▭ purple   ○ yellow

How many equal parts?

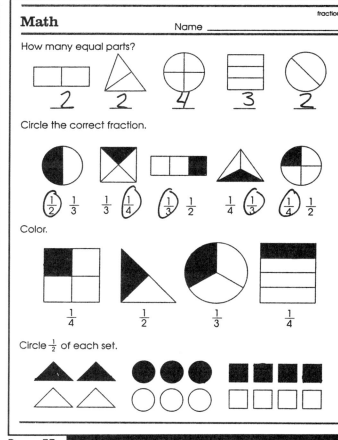

Circle the correct fraction.

Color.

Circle $\frac{1}{2}$ of each set.

Add.

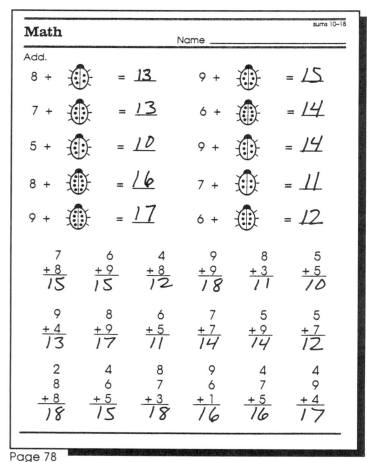

8 + 🐞 = **13**   9 + 🐞 = **15**
7 + 🐞 = **13**   6 + 🐞 = **14**
5 + 🐞 = **10**   9 + 🐞 = **14**
8 + 🐞 = **16**   7 + 🐞 = **11**
9 + 🐞 = **17**   6 + 🐞 = **12**

7	6	4	9	8	5
+8	+9	+8	+9	+3	+5
15	**15**	**12**	**18**	**11**	**10**

9	8	6	7	5	5
+4	+9	+5	+7	+9	+7
13	**17**	**11**	**14**	**14**	**12**

2	4	8	9	4	4
8	6	7	6	7	9
+8	+5	+3	+1	+5	+4
18	**15**	**18**	**16**	**16**	**17**

Write the subtraction sentences.

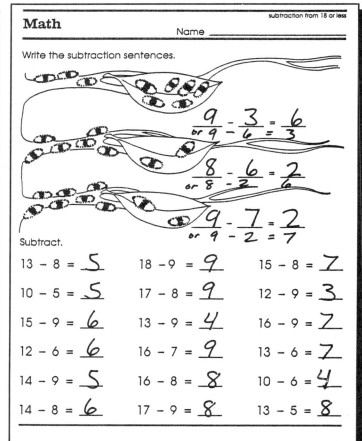

$\frac{9 - 3 = 6}{\text{or } 9 - 6 = 3}$

$\frac{8 - 6 = 2}{\text{or } 8 - 2 = 6}$

$\frac{9 - 7 = 2}{\text{or } 9 - 2 = 7}$

Subtract.

13 − 8 = **5**   18 − 9 = **9**   15 − 8 = **7**
10 − 5 = **5**   17 − 8 = **9**   12 − 9 = **3**
15 − 9 = **6**   13 − 9 = **4**   16 − 9 = **7**
12 − 6 = **6**   16 − 7 = **9**   13 − 6 = **7**
14 − 9 = **5**   16 − 8 = **8**   10 − 6 = **4**
14 − 8 = **6**   17 − 9 = **8**   13 − 5 = **8**

Page 80

Name _____

Solve.

6 +			16 –			13 –	
6 =	12		9 =	7		8 =	5
3 =	9		5 =	11		5 =	8
9 =	15		6 =	10		9 =	4
4 =	10		3 =	13		7 =	6
8 =	14		8 =	8		3 =	10
2 =	8		2 =	14		4 =	9

8 +			18 –			7 +	
7 =	15		9 =	9		9 =	16
1 =	9		4 =	14		1 =	8
9 =	17		1 =	17		8 =	15
6 =	14		8 =	10		7 =	14
4 =	12		5 =	13		2 =	9
2 =	10		7 =	11		5 =	12
8 =	16		3 =	15		4 =	11

Page 81

Name _____

Write two addition and two subtraction facts for each number family.

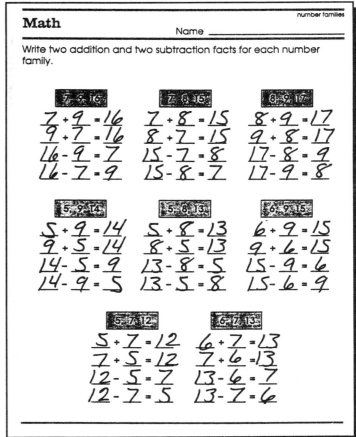

7 9 16
$7 + 9 = 16$
$9 + 7 = 16$
$16 - 9 = 7$
$16 - 7 = 9$

7 8 15
$7 + 8 = 15$
$8 + 7 = 15$
$15 - 7 = 8$
$15 - 8 = 7$

8 9 17
$8 + 9 = 17$
$9 + 8 = 17$
$17 - 8 = 9$
$17 - 9 = 8$

5 9 14
$5 + 9 = 14$
$9 + 5 = 14$
$14 - 5 = 9$
$14 - 9 = 5$

5 8 13
$5 + 8 = 13$
$8 + 5 = 13$
$13 - 8 = 5$
$13 - 5 = 8$

6 9 15
$6 + 9 = 15$
$9 + 6 = 15$
$15 - 9 = 6$
$15 - 6 = 9$

5 7 12
$5 + 7 = 12$
$7 + 5 = 12$
$12 - 5 = 7$
$12 - 7 = 5$

6 7 13
$6 + 7 = 13$
$7 + 6 = 13$
$13 - 6 = 7$
$13 - 7 = 6$

Page 82

Name _____

Write the addition or subtraction sentence.

You had 6. You earned 5. How many cents do you have in all? **11¢**	You had 8. You found 6. How many cents do you have in all? **14¢**
You had 15. You lost 6. How many cents do you have left? **9¢**	You had 13. You gave away 7. How many cents do you have left? **6¢**
You bought 8 apples. You bought 9. How many in all? **17**	You bought 12 bananas. You ate 7. How many do you have left? **5**
You saw 13 apples. 6 were red. How many were not red? **7**	You bought 9 pears. You bought 6 more. How many did you buy in all? **15**
You picked 7 flowers. You picked 8 more. How many did you pick all together? **15**	You bought 14 lollipops. You ate 5. How many do you have left? **9**

Page 83

Name _____

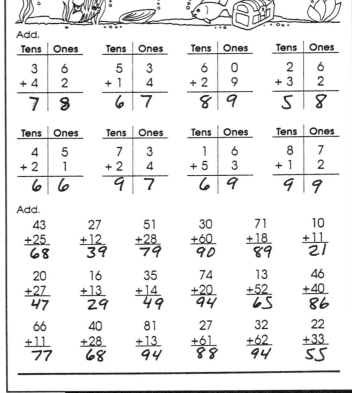

Add.

Tens	Ones		Tens	Ones		Tens	Ones		Tens	Ones
3	6		5	3		6	0		2	6
+ 4	2		+ 1	4		+ 2	9		+ 3	2
7	8		6	7		8	9		5	8

Tens	Ones		Tens	Ones		Tens	Ones		Tens	Ones
4	5		7	3		1	6		8	7
+ 2	1		+ 2	4		+ 5	3		+ 1	2
6	6		9	7		6	9		9	9

Add.

43 +25 **68**	27 +12 **39**	51 +28 **79**	30 +60 **90**	71 +18 **89**	10 +11 **21**
20 +27 **47**	16 +13 **29**	35 +14 **49**	74 +20 **94**	13 +52 **65**	46 +40 **86**
66 +11 **77**	40 +28 **68**	81 +13 **94**	27 +61 **88**	32 +62 **94**	22 +33 **55**

Page 84

Math

two-digit subtraction: no regrouping

Name _____

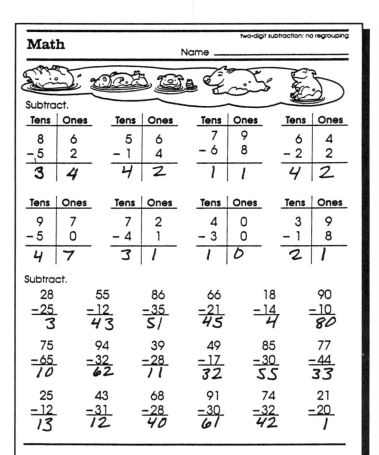

Subtract.

Tens	Ones
8	6
– 5	2
3	**4**

Tens	Ones
5	6
– 1	4
4	**2**

Tens	Ones
7	9
– 6	8
1	**1**

Tens	Ones
6	4
– 2	2
4	**2**

Tens	Ones
9	7
– 5	0
4	**7**

Tens	Ones
7	2
– 4	1
3	**1**

Tens	Ones
4	0
– 3	0
1	**0**

Tens	Ones
3	9
– 1	8
2	**1**

Subtract.

28	55	86	66	18	90
–25	–12	–35	–21	–14	–10
3	**43**	**51**	**45**	**4**	**80**

75	94	39	49	85	77
–65	–32	–28	–17	–30	–44
10	**62**	**11**	**32**	**55**	**33**

25	43	68	91	74	21
–12	–31	–28	–30	–32	–20
13	**12**	**40**	**61**	**42**	**1**

Page 84

Page 85

Math

two-digit addition and subtraction

Name _____

Add or subtract.

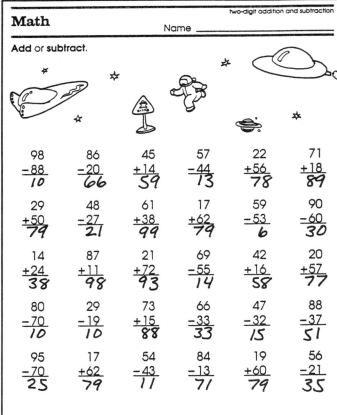

98	86	45	57	22	71
–88	–20	+14	–44	+56	+18
10	**66**	**59**	**13**	**78**	**89**

29	48	61	17	59	90
+50	–27	+38	+62	–53	–60
79	**21**	**99**	**79**	**6**	**30**

14	87	21	69	42	20
+24	+11	+72	–55	+16	+57
38	**98**	**93**	**14**	**58**	**77**

80	29	73	66	47	88
–70	–19	+15	–33	–32	–37
10	**10**	**88**	**33**	**15**	**51**

95	17	54	84	19	56
–70	+62	–43	–13	+60	–21
25	**79**	**11**	**71**	**79**	**35**

Page 85

Page 86

Math

problem solving: mixed addition and subtraction

Name _____

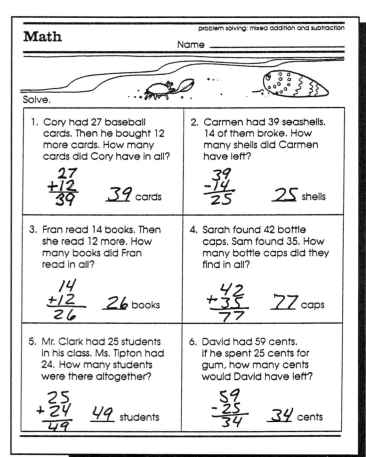

Solve.

1. Cory had 27 baseball cards. Then he bought 12 more cards. How many cards did Cory have in all?

$$\begin{array}{r} 27 \\ +12 \\ \hline 39 \end{array}$$ **39** cards

2. Carmen had 39 seashells. 14 of them broke. How many shells did Carmen have left?

$$\begin{array}{r} 39 \\ -14 \\ \hline 25 \end{array}$$ **25** shells

3. Fran read 14 books. Then she read 12 more. How many books did Fran read in all?

$$\begin{array}{r} 14 \\ +12 \\ \hline 26 \end{array}$$ **26** books

4. Sarah found 42 bottle caps. Sam found 35. How many bottle caps did they find in all?

$$\begin{array}{r} 42 \\ +35 \\ \hline 77 \end{array}$$ **77** caps

5. Mr. Clark had 25 students in his class. Ms. Tipton had 24. How many students were there altogether?

$$\begin{array}{r} 25 \\ +24 \\ \hline 49 \end{array}$$ **49** students

6. David had 59 cents. If he spent 25 cents for gum, how many cents would David have left?

$$\begin{array}{r} 59 \\ -25 \\ \hline 34 \end{array}$$ **34** cents

Page 86

Page 87

Health and Science

nutrition: classifying

Name _____

Make wise food choices by using the food group pyramid. Study the pyramid. Complete the exercises.

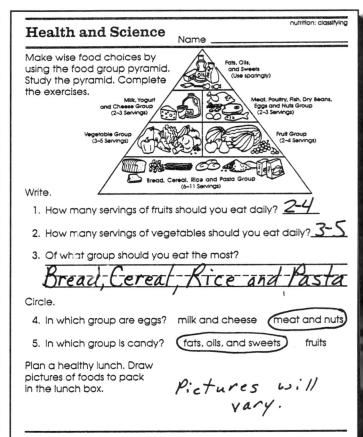

Write.

1. How many servings of fruits should you eat daily? **2-4**

2. How many servings of vegetables should you eat daily? **3-5**

3. Of what group should you eat the most?

Bread, Cereal, Rice and Pasta

Circle.

4. In which group are eggs?   milk and cheese   (**meat and nuts**)

5. In which group is candy?   (**fats, oils, and sweets**)   fruits

Plan a healthy lunch. Draw pictures of foods to pack in the lunch box.

Pictures will vary.

Page 87

© Instructional Fair, Inc.   124   IF8783 First Grade in Review

Health and Science

Name _____

Write a sentence to tell about something you remember doing as a baby.

Answer will vary.

Write about something you can do now.

Answer will vary.

Cut and paste the pictures below to answer the questions.

a. What could a baby do?

b. What could a child do?

c. What could an adult do?

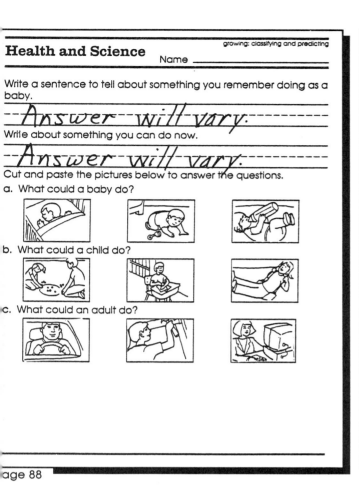

Health and Science

Name _____

Write the name of the home in which each animal lives. Use the words from the Word Box.

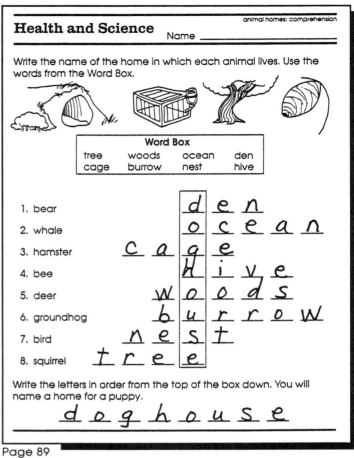

Word Box			
tree	woods	ocean	den
cage	burrow	nest	hive

1. bear — d e n
2. whale — o c e a n
3. hamster — c a g e
4. bee — h i v e
5. deer — w o o d s
6. groundhog — b u r r o w
7. bird — n e s t
8. squirrel — t r e e

Write the letters in order from the top of the box down. You will name a home for a puppy.

d o g h o u s e

Health and Science

Name _____

Color each picture that shows a way to help the environment. Draw an **X** on those that do not.

Health and Science

Name _____

Draw a line to match the words with the correct picture.

1. A butterfly lays an egg on a leaf.

2. A caterpillar comes out of the egg. It eats and eats.

3. The caterpillar spins a cocoon. Inside, the caterpillar becomes a pupa.

4. A butterfly comes out of the cocoon. It dries its wings and flies away.

Cut and paste the pictures on the circle in the correct order to show the life cycle of a butterfly.

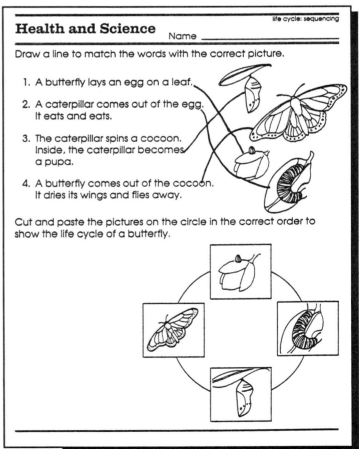

---

125   IF8783 First Grade in Review

Name _____

heat: predicting

Match the pictures on the left with those on the right to show how heat changes things.

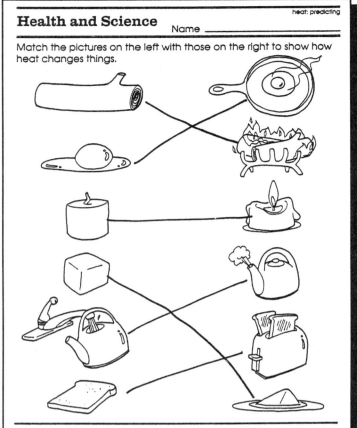

Health and Science Name _____

safety: comprehension

Color the picture in each set that shows a way to be safe. Draw an X on the one that is not safe.

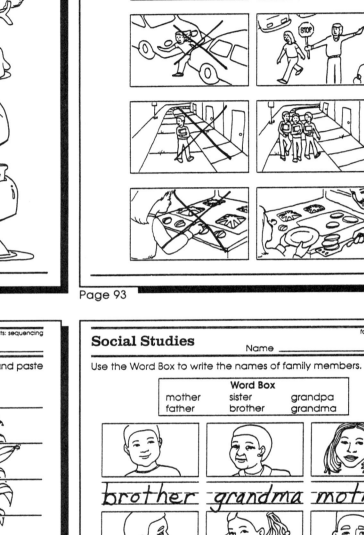

Health and Science Name _____

plants: sequencing

Read the sentence strips at the bottom of the page. Cut and paste them in the correct order on the lines.

The seed of corn is planted in good soil.

The baby plant sprouts.

The plant grows taller and ears of corn form.

The ears of corn are ready to pick.

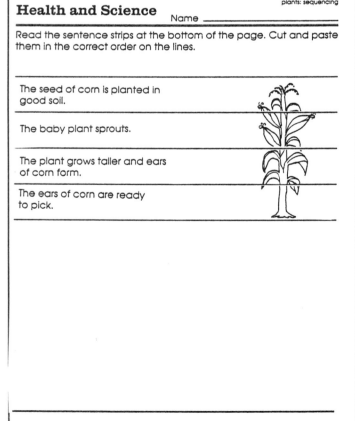

Social Studies Name _____

families: classifying

Use the Word Box to write the names of family members.

Word Box		
mother	sister	grandpa
father	brother	grandma

brother   grandma   mother

grandpa   sister   father

Color the pictures that show how family members help each other.

Social Studies

Name _____

All people **need** food, clothing, shelter, and love. Sometimes people **want** other things as well.

Draw a line through the row that shows three things people **need**.

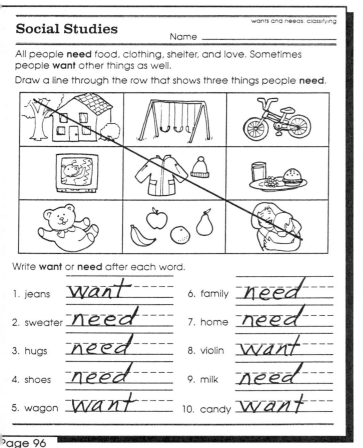

Write **want** or **need** after each word.

1. jeans   *want*
2. sweater   *need*
3. hugs   *need*
4. shoes   *need*
5. wagon   *want*

6. family   *need*
7. home   *need*
8. violin   *want*
9. milk   *need*
10. candy   *want*

Social Studies

Name _____

Write the name of the worker under the picture. Use the Word Box.

Word Box

| farmer | painter | teacher |
| pilot | nurse | bus driver |

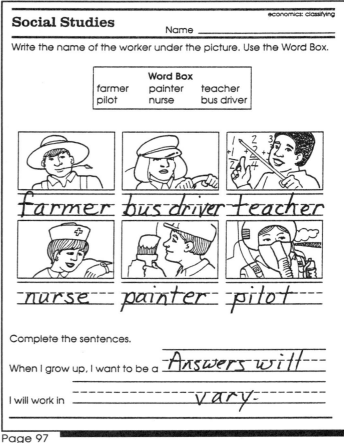

farmer   *bus driver*   *teacher*

nurse   *painter*   *pilot*

Complete the sentences.

When I grow up, I want to be a _*Answers will*_

I will work in _____ *vary.*

Social Studies

Name _____

In the boxes below, **color** only the pictures of **groups**.

Rules help groups work together. Check the rules that help groups work together.

✓ 1. Take turns talking.
✓ 2. Listen carefully.
✓ 3. Share ideas.

____ 4. Everyone talk at once.
✓ 5. Share the work.
✓ 6. Be polite.

Social Studies

Name _____

North, **south**, **east**, and **west** are directions.

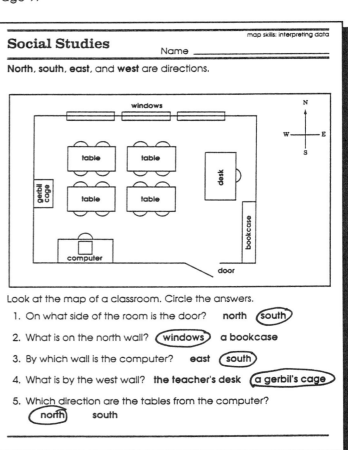

Look at the map of a classroom. Circle the answers.

1. On what side of the room is the door?   **north**   (south)
2. What is on the north wall?   (windows)   a bookcase
3. By which wall is the computer?   **east**   (south)
4. What is by the west wall?   **the teacher's desk**   (a gerbil's cage)
5. Which direction are the tables from the computer?
   (north)   south

Social Studies

Name _____

This is a map of Nick's neighborhood. Use the **key** to answer the questions.

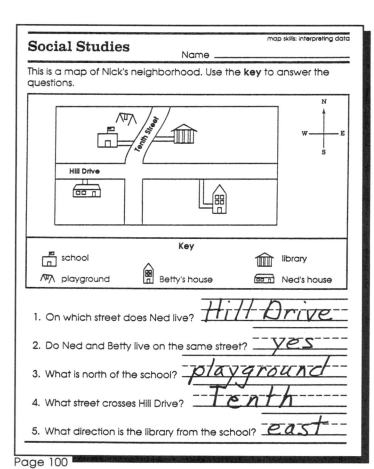

Key

🏫 school   🏛 library

🛝 playground   🏠 Betty's house   🏘 Ned's house

1. On which street does Ned live? *Hill Drive*

2. Do Ned and Betty live on the same street? *yes*

3. What is north of the school? *playground*

4. What street crosses Hill Drive? *Tenth*

5. What direction is the library from the school? *east*

Page 100

Social Studies

Name _____

Read the chart to find out how Abraham Lincoln and John F. Kennedy were alike and different. Use the information to answer the questions.

Abraham Lincoln	John F. Kennedy
was poor as a child	was rich as a child
loved to read	loved to read
had a good sense of humor	had a good sense of humor
the father of three sons	the father of a boy and a girl
became President of the U.S.	became President of the U.S.
was shot and killed	was shot and killed

1. In how many ways were Abraham Lincoln and John F. Kennedy alike? *4*

2. Which man was rich as a child? *Kennedy*

3. Which man had more children? *Lincoln*

4. Which man had a daughter? *Kennedy*

Write the name of the person who is President now.

Answers will vary by year.

Page 101

Social Studies

Name _____

Holidays are special days which some people celebrate. Match the picture with the name of the holiday.

Hanukkah

Christmas

Halloween

Fourth of July

Thanksgiving

Martin Luther King, Jr. Day

Easter

Write two sentences about a holiday you celebrate.

Answers will vary.

Page 102

About the Book

This is a great activity book which can be used in the spring for review, or in the summer or fall to brush up on skills from the previous year. The author has used a variety of activities which every child will enjoy while reviewing Language Arts, Math, Health and Science and Social Studies.

Credits

Author: Sally Fisk
Artist: Marie Marfia
Project Director/Editor: Sue Sutton
Editors: Alyson Kieda, Rhonda DeWaard
*Cover Photo: Frank Pieroni
Production: Pat Geasler

*Cover photo taken of the Rounds School in Rockford, MI. Permission to use given by the Rockford Rotary Club.